SUMMERS AND SABBATICALS

SUMMERS AND SABBATICALS

Selected Papers on Psychology and Education

FRED S. KELLER

32180

Research Press Company
2612 North Mattis Avenue • Champaign, Illinois 61820

ISBN 0-87822-134-4

Library of Congress Catalog Card Number 76-52355

To Frances, Anne, and John,
for their forbearance.

Contents

Foreword

When the *Journal of the Experimental Analysis of Behavior* was founded in 1958, the first paper in the first issue was "The Phantom Plateau" by F. S. Keller. When the *Journal of Applied Behavior Analysis* was founded ten years later, the first issue contained a paper called "Goodbye Teacher . . ." by the same author. These facts have a symbolic touch. Keller has always been in at the beginning of things.

"The Phantom Plateau" disposed of some experiments which had characterized an early epoch in learning theory. The paper converted the learning-curve-with-plateau into something like the two-line joke that the *New Yorker* used to run once a year to remind its readers of how styles in humor had changed. "Goodbye Teacher . . ." was a manifesto, announcing a new era in higher education which is only just beginning to be understood on a scale commensurate with its importance.

To say that Keller is an initiator, an originator, a creator may seem to violate the behavioristic contention that no one really starts anything, and a biographer in possession of all the facts could no doubt trace what he has done to details of his genetic and personal histories, but so far as the scientific study of behavior in America is concerned, the important thing is the achievement itself. No one has more consistently furthered an experimental analysis of behavior or clarified its implications. Impatient with the commonplace, the standard, the too readily accepted, he has broken into new and exciting fields and has taken a host of others with him. He is a prospector who has never staked a claim but who has shown many others where the gold is to be found.

Keller seems to get more fun out of his work than most speakers or writers. As these papers make clear, he is a master of the low-key. He will begin a lecture as if apologizing for his appearance on the platform; the audience drops its defenses and is easily captured. But the rhetorical strategy is evidently used just for the fun of it. The message is there, supported by a wealth of evidence, and would have been convincing no matter how it was presented. And so, a word of caution: let readers who dismiss some of these papers as of merely passing interest beware! They may learn more from them than they think.

Harvard University   B. F. Skinner

Preface

This book comprises about one-quarter of the papers I have written within a span of forty years. I blush when I compare my output with that of almost any colleague in a major university, but I tell myself that I have been primarily a teacher, rather than a research worker or a textbook author. Summers and sabbaticals were the principal times I had for writing and experimentation. Most of the contributions to this book were written in those periods of recreation and refueling.

The papers I have brought together here are parts of a continued story. I discovered this while sorting out my reprints. Although each separate endeavor seemed at the time to be in answer to external pressures only, this was not entirely true. I found a meaningful progression in my work that I had not seen before. Each contribution, looked at closely, was part of a larger whole.

There were other things I found when I examined my production, not all of which enhanced my self-esteem. I have been concerned with *individual organisms,* for example. My doctoral research had four white rats as subjects, and in my later animal studies the number was seldom greater. The code-voice method of radio-operator training was developed with one person at a time, and three students provided an ethnic mix in my first approach to personalized instruction. Any groups with which I may have worked were usually in collaborative studies. I trace all this to my lack of grounding in statistics and to the model of research at Harvard in my years of study there.

I have *avoided complex apparatus.* Wooden mazes were the first (and only) devices that I constructed for experimental use, and I never learned to operate anything more intricate than a commercial Skinner Box or a telegraph key and sounder. I blame this on the fact that I was born in the horse-and-buggy days, when the most complicated thing with which I had to cope was a bicycle with a coaster brake. There may of course be deeper explanations.

A related bias can be found in my dependence on *simple methods* of training, teaching, and experimental research. This stems in large part, too, from my ignorance of statistics. If one doesn't feel secure with such devices, he must find a simpler way of getting where he wants to go.

Finally, I have been a *leaner*. I have depended on my colleagues and my pupils for things I couldn't do alone. It seems to me that I have been the Great Exploiter with respect to theory as well as practical skills; and I ask myself if there is anything within these pages that is peculiarly my own. My debt to Burrhus Skinner is no secret, but there were many others, some of whom are cited in this book. Among those who helped me most, four names stand out: Spaulding Rogers, W. N. Schoenfeld, John Volkmann, and Rodolfo Azzi. I leaned on each in different ways, but each was vitally important to me. I am glad to have this chance to acknowledge their support.

1

Psychology at Harvard (1926-1931) A Reminiscence

This paper was written as an invited contribution to the *Festschrift for B. F. Skinner* (Appleton-Century-Crofts, 1970); material was collected and prepared for publication by P. B. Dews and a committee composed of Charles A. Catania and Victor G. Laties. The content of this paper, rather than its date of publication, dictated its position as my leadoff item.

This paper is reprinted from *Festschrift for B. F. Skinner,* P. B. Dews, et al, Appleton-Century-Crofts, 1970. It is reprinted with permission from P. B. Dews.

Harvard University, in the late twenties of this century, was not the only center of American psychology. Yale, Pennsylvania, Cornell, Clark, Chicago, Princeton, Columbia, California (Berkeley), Stanford, and Minnesota boasted good departments, as did a few other universities. But Harvard was important—important in the eyes of the scholarly world, of its carefully chosen staff, and of each little band of students admitted yearly to its graduate classes. It may not have been the most American of psychology departments, but it was probably the most prestigious.

Admission to graduate study within its halls was not a complicated matter or fraught with undue worry. Applicants were few and decisions were made without the pretence of measuring a candidate's potentiality for success. A letter of recommendation, a personal introduction to the Chairman (with a few words of supporting comment), and an interview of perhaps five minutes' duration, were enough to launch a career. One had to have his A.B., or B.S., but not necessarily with distinction or in a special field of study. "We'll try to make an experimentalist out of you," said the Chairman, and one's acceptance was assured.

To a young man with a bad secondary-school education and a baccalaureate of dubious quality from a small New England college, Harvard was nevertheless a frightening place, once classes had begun. Not just because of its Yard, its ivied brick and classic columns, or academic fame; not just because of the forbidding silence and pervasive gloom of Emerson Hall, where one climbed daily to the third-floor home of the Department; but also because of an indefinable atmosphere, a certain ectoplasm of erudition, remoteness, and austerity that exuded from the Staff itself—from the directors of one's destiny.

As I call them up now in free association, they were an impressive group. Professor Boring, our Head, our principal lecturer, our mentor, and our conscience, was able to excite our respect, affection, fear, and amusement, in roughly that rank order of frequency. His were the unofficial *core* courses, rich in content and presented with the same compelling animation, semester after semester, at the same morning hour. Under him we studied *history, sensation, perception,* and *association and determination.* For none of these was there a textbook, so we sometimes came early to class to copy the suggested readings from the blackboard. Since many of these references were in German, we relied heavily upon our lecture notes in satisfying course requirements.

Professor Pratt, a Quaker, like Boring, who had come with the latter from Clark, seemed as much at home in art as in science, in German as in English. He lectured, sometimes explosively, in beautifully resonant tones that always commanded attention; and he had, as I recall it, some skill in vocal mimicry. (I seem to remember an impressive imitation of suction-cup

3

tires on a wet pavement.) Through him I was introduced (barely) to *psychophysics* and, in a term of *aesthetics,* came to enjoy Santayana.

Professor Troland, once called "the young Helmholtz," excited our awe and admiration not by his lectures, which were sleep inducing, but by his many textbooks, "written from dictation," someone said, "like Edgar Wallace mysteries," and by his recognition in the practical world of Technicolor. His knowledge seemed encyclopaedic, his laboratory a marvel of mirrors, tubes, and lenses, and his manner shy to the extreme. (I'll never forget our mutual embarrassment when, following a Christmas recess, I met him in the hallway, loaded down with mail, and impulsively extended my hand in greeting.) I attended his lectures on *physiological psychology* and *motivation,* and his evening seminar on *vision.*

Professor Beebe-Center was impressive, too, and not just because of the hyphen. Tall and slightly stooped, always running away in his manner, he spoke French "like a native," was said to have a chateau in Tours, to teach at Harvard simply *pour le sport,* and to turn back his salary regularly to the University. He was also warm and responsive, but this I did not know for several years. With him I spent a term on *affectivity* (thus catalogued in deference to Radcliffe's Dean, for whom *affection* had improper overtones), while he was writing his *Pleasantness and Unpleasantness.* Beebe-Center was crystal clear in classroom exposition and unusually stimulative of research, even by undergraduates. He graded our French and German, too.

Professor Murray, at the Clinic, was the most approachable of all, seeming to welcome lecture interruptions and the exchange of ideas with students. He was, of course, not a *real* psychologist, like those of Emerson Hall, being interested in such concepts as *thematic apperception,* such measuring devices as the *psychogalvanic reflex,* and such an area of study as that of unconscious motivation. He had an M.D. from Columbia, a Ph.D. from Cambridge, and rumor gave him "a wealthy Back Bay private practice." He was a provocative person, with a twinkling eye and an endearing speech defect, and I liked him very much, but he was clearly of a foreign population.

These were the central figures in our citadel of learning. Upon their teachings we depended most in passing two of our three main examinations on the way to our doctorates—the written "prelims" and the oral "general." Their courses would later serve as models, or at least as starting points, for courses of our own. From them we would draw not only facts and theories, but anecdotes and gossip, as well as our classroom styles.

They did, indeed, leave their marks upon us. Even now, more than forty years later, I can see Professor Boring, eyes rolled upwards, shoulders hunched, palms together before him, marching to and fro, with occasional darting smiles in our direction, as he explained Korte's Laws, praised Heymans' approach to the Mueller-Lyer problem, summarized John Locke on the qualities of objects, distinguished between *Kundgabe* and *Beschreibung,* and discussed Rubin on figure-ground, Helmholtz on unconscious inference, Johannes Mueller on specific nerve energies, or G. E. Mueller on the method of *right associates.*

I can see Professor Troland, a study in preoccupation, discoursing in monotone on *retroflex* action (and smiling faintly as he disclaimed a personal reference in the *tro* of retroflex); on the relation of *P* and *U* to synaptic resistance; and on the merits of the three hedonisms—of the past, the present, and the future. I can also see Professor Beebe-Center, concernedly evaluating the tridimensional theory of feeling or the existence of an indifference point on the *P-U* continuum; Professor Pratt, showing us, with the aid of a recording, the lack of resolution in *Tristan and Isolde,* or illustrating the accrual of *context* to *core* by vocalizing

> When fur stews can the sill Lear I'm
> Toot rye tomb ache the mean ink leer
> Yule thin kits own lea way sting thyme . . . . etc.;

and Professor Murray, relating self-assertive to self-corrective compulsions, or introducing to his class a middle-aged nurse with "automatic speech." These and many other scenes are readily reinstated and they bring, I must confess, a certain nostalgia with them.

These men were not the only ones to whom I was, or could have been, exposed in the late twenties. Nearby, in physiology, was Professor Crozier, reputedly addicted to who-dun-its, working in the Loeb tradition and exciting the behaviorally inclined among us who were not mathematically illiterate. At the Medical School, there were Professors Davis and Forbes, for those who wanted the latest in nervous-system function and were hardy enough for the cross-town trip. Professor Dearborn was accessible, but seldom used, in education and statistics; Professor Sarton could be enjoyed (in the History of Science) without leaving Emerson Hall, as could Professors Whitehead, Perry, and a few other philosophers and logicians. We had a bountiful fare which, unfortunately, my own early training did not fully prepare me to appreciate.

Then there were our Visiting Professors, who spent a Summer Session with us, or even a regular term or two. I remember with especial pleasure the classes of Professors Hunter (Clark), Tolman (Berkeley), Perrin (Texas), and Buehler (Vienna). Koffka was also there from Smith, Robinson from Chicago, and Stone from Stanford, but I had no room for them within my workday schedule. None of the men under whom I did sit was very skilled at the podium; they excited me, I think, because they told about their unsolved problems, exposed their half-formed theories, and encouraged us to struggle with each. Our regular mentors were impressive in their scholarship, but commonly left us gasping with all that we had to learn; there was little time for thinking.

Professor Buehler, an expressive and *gemuetvoll* person, brought us his theory of language, with a strong European flavor and some special English-language problems of his own. Professors Tolman, Hunter, and Perrin brought us animal researches, principally maze-learning studies, and provided us with our first respectable, academic taste of behaviorism. What's more, they gave us a glimpse of a fresh, free-swinging, non-Wundtian, "Western" world, in which teachers sometimes hobnobbed with students, in which issues were debated at kitchen-table seminars over mugs of prohibition beer, and where scholarship was probably defective (from our cloistered point of view), but where something new and possibly significant was stirring. For a few of us, their influence was actually greater than that of our regular staff.

Also a part of our educational scene was a long line of short-time visitors who came to give an address (e.g., a Lowell Lecture), to speak at our Colloquium, to attend the 1927 meeting of the Society of Experimental Psychologists, or simply to visit the laboratories. I recall, in particular, talks by W. B. Cannon, on emotion and bodily changes (dull); Selig Hecht, on visual theory (brilliantly impressive, he made you want to be a scientist); A. V. Hill, on fatigue (impressively British); L. Lapicque, on chronaxie (very French, but quite clear); Wolfgang Koehler, on "insight" (charming, but elusive); K. S. Lashley, on brain extirpation and maze learning (ghoulish); John Paul Nafe, on feeling (sepulchral); Johnson O'Connor, on aptitude testing (wrong audience); and J. B. Rhine, McDougall's assistant, agonizedly defending his chief's position on the Lamarckian inheritance of maze-swimming skill in the rat.

I can remember Professor McDougall himself, marching down the corridor, a short and chesty Roman senator, with a former pupil in tow; Professors Dallenbach and Langfeld, conversing in an empty classroom, Van Dykes wagging; and Professor Titchener ("T"), a stern little Santa, unconsciously presiding over his Society's meeting as Harold Schlosberg, a young graduate student from Princeton, reported his work on knee-jerk conditioning (to be tagged immediately as a "biological" study by the unofficial Chairman).

We saw our regular professors mainly in the classroom, or at Colloquium over tea and coffee. The atmosphere was never unfriendly, but there was little social interaction between the students and the staff. In five years of half-time study at Harvard, I was twice at Professor Boring's home, and once, I believe, at Professor Pratt's. On the two or three occasions when I conferred with Professor Boring in his office, it was under pressure from the timer on his desk, which could abruptly end our meeting. No one of the teachers I have mentioned ever called me by my given name, and I, of course, was never less formal than "Professor" or "Doctor"—a habit that was not really shaken in my later contacts with them.

With some of the younger men, at the instructor level, we enjoyed an easier relationship, especially as we neared the end of our studies. Frank Pattie, tall, languid, and suspected of genius, permitted "Frank"; Morgan Upton was "Kelly" to everyone who worked in the new animal laboratory at the top of Boylston Hall; and M. H. Elliott, a Tolman Ph.D., whom I assisted in Undergraduate Experimental, was "Hugh" to me and several others. Such intimacy was rare, however, and seldom led further than coffee together at the Georgian. The roles of teacher and pupil, master and apprentice, senior and junior, or worker and player, were clearly discriminated in the twenties.

When I ask myself what *students* I knew at Harvard during the time that I was there, I find that I'm in trouble. There were many more of them than teachers, and both the quality and quantity of my relations with them varied through a wider range. In a couple of hours, I was able to list the names of about thirty comrades-in-study[1] with whom I had some contact in the years between 1926 and 1931. Within this group, there were fifteen or twenty whom I knew quite well from having sat in class with them regularly, worked with them on laboratory exercises, or studied with them for examinations; and, finally, there were eight or ten of these whom I learned to know intimately through extracurricular connections of one sort or another—at mealtimes, in the evenings, or on social safaris. Especially memorable are the hours I spent with Wes Bousfield, Jim Coronios, Paul Huston, Mac McCarthy, Obie Oberlin, Burrhus Skinner,[2] Bill Turner, and Jack Volkmann. (Briefer association was enjoyed with Hyung Lin Kim, Ed Newbury, Muzafer Sherif, and Bill Stavsky.)[3]

These men differed greatly in their origins and in their destinies. Of the former I can say little, but I know they ended up in widely different *ambientes.* Bousfield, Coronios, Newbury, Sherif, Skinner, and Volkmann remained in academic psychology; Huston went on to psychiatry and adminstration, with a medical degree; Oberlin soon turned from teaching to counselling and psychotherapy; Stavsky became a clinician; Turner's interests shifted to social work and administration; Kim went into business; and McCarthy, I believe, went into ophthalmology. Oddly enough, from a Department dedicated to the furtherance of normal, adult, human, experimental psychology in the classical tradition, Bousfield and Volkmann alone have borne the standard of such a science throughout their

7

long and productive careers. A similar ratio holds when the larger group is considered.

When I am asked to talk about my days at Harvard, the focal point of interest is sometimes not exclusively in Harvard or my days, but in Burrhus Frederic Skinner and what I knew about him when we were there together. This is understandable. Among all of us who walked the Yard to Emerson and Boylston Halls in the twenties, he is the one whose name is known around the world today. Moreover, he has mentioned me in print on several occasions and honored me with a textbook dedication, while I have paid homage to his genius at various times and places. It is no wonder that strangers ask me about the relationship between us; that loyal pupils sometimes imagine influences upon him that I never exercised; that unfriendly critics cry "disciple," or worse; and that curious colleagues look to me for "inside" stories. (Sometimes I am even asked to defend the mode of life in *Walden Two,* discuss the "baby box" in pediatric detail, or give the *coup de grace* to Dr. Chomsky.)

I don't know where or when I first met Burrhus Skinner. Let us just say in a Harvard classroom, in 1928; I doubt that anyone will check. And it could not have been long thereafter when he rented basement quarters in the Arlington Street apartment house in which I lived. From then on, we began to see each other fairly often, and discovered a number of things we had in common.

Our tastes in food, for example. Each of us had been sensitized by travel abroad, especially in Paris. I remember a good onion soup that we concocted in our kitchen, aiming, I suppose, to recover Left Bank savors; and the time when my friend bought a keg of wine-to-be, which was delivered with full instructions for aging, but which never really grew to vintage stature. Best of all, I remember excursions to Boston, by subway, to favorite eating places. We went to Jake Wirth's for *bratwurst and shell beans, sauerbraten, apfel strudel,* and other delicacies, topped off with seidels of point-three beer, in a high-ceilinged room with sawdust on the floor, *Suum Quique* over the bar, and the good-natured service of harried waiters who sometimes recognized our faces. We went to the Athens-Olympia, also on Stuart Street, for chicken *pilaf,* strong dark wine (presumably "needled") in coffee cups, and *baklava;* or to Locke-Ober's, dressed for the occasion, at a window table on the street floor (for gentlemen only), where we had dishes with sherry in them and chatted like true cosmopolites. Less lavishly, but more frequently, we enjoyed a simple Chinese meal, with chopsticks, in a little upstairs place near Harvard Square.

We each liked bicycling and we bought two Columbia wheels, which our boyhood expertise had recommended as the best. We often rode them to work and sometimes took trips together. We went to Walden Pond, where we stood beside the pile of stones that were thought to mark the site of Thoreau's hut, and talked about *Life in the Woods*. Our longest journey was to Providence, for an overnight stay at Brown, where Charley Trueblood and Jim Coronios were doing their doctoral research. My bike was finally stolen, from in front of Boylston Hall; I don't know what happened to his.

On a less positive note, there were other sources of affinity. Each of us had resisted parental wishes in choosing a vocation; each had openly renounced his early religious teachings; each had attacked such college prescriptions as "physical education" and compulsory chapel attendance; each had felt himself out of step with his fellow undergraduates; and each was as "un-American" as he could be without endangering any of his basic rights or privileges. (We didn't wear attention-getting costumes; we didn't march in the streets for Sacco and Vanzetti; we didn't join our expatriate contemporaries in Paris; we didn't burn our college diplomas; and we didn't even buy the *American Mercury* openly on Boston Common, in defiance of the Watch and Ward Society. I would say that we were *tamely* un-American, not at all like our present-day "activists.")

We were also budding *behaviorists*, in a department that was basically structuralistic. Skinner had read Pavlov, Loeb, and Watson (*Behaviorism*) before coming to Harvard, and I had been led back into college in 1925 by reading *Psychology from the Standpoint of a Behaviorist*. We defended the position in many lively debates with our peers and occasionally spoke out in the classroom. I was greatly flattered once when Professor Murray referred to us as "lions in debate." I should probably have been embarrassed, but psychology in the twenties was not yet the experimental science that it is today. The relative merits of the various *schools* were still of major concern to anyone who planned, as we did, to spend his life in teaching.

So much for the things we shared. I haven't included them all, and I don't mean to suggest that we shared them exclusively. Each of us had his own sociogram, which included friends who never met each other. And it should go without saying that there were many other things which we did not have in common. Besides the obvious difference in genetic constitution, we were brought up on different sides of the track, we had different occupational histories, military experience, and quality of education. We enjoyed different kinds of prose and poetry, had liked different kinds of music, had felt differently about competitive sports, and had fallen in love with different types of girls. Had we been reared in the same town, we might never have met.

We had very different patterns of work and play. At nine in the morning, when I was still rubbing sleep from my eyes, his working day was well advanced; but he was no good at all socially after nine in the evening, when I was wide awake. It used to irritate me mildly to see him playing pingong with Bill Stavsky or some other denizen of Boylston Hall in the middle of the "working day," and I was faintly annoyed that he found time to play the piano or make marionettes for Hallowell Davis's children. I don't know how we had as many hours together as we did.

In view of the fact that most of my academic life has since been spent in the advancement of reinforcement theory and its application, it may seem strange that my real interest in "Skinnerian" research did not begin at Harvard in the twenties, when my friend was developing his experimental techniques, collecting early data, and starting to build a system. The fact is, however, that it didn't, and, at the risk of too much self-reference, I'll try to explain why.

First, in addition to my teaching and laboratory duties, I had my doctoral research to look after (a follow-up of Hunter's work with the temporal maze), a dissertation to write (without an active sponsor), and examinations to pass. This left me with little time for thinking about the work of other graduate students. (Actually, Skinner took more account of my research than I of his. Observing my tedious daily task of running rats, he once constructed an automatic temporal maze that would permit an animal to carry out a left-left-right-right sequence of choices twenty-four hours a day, receiving all his food and drink within the apparatus. Had the procedure been successful, I would probably have had to alter my theory of the learning process involved. More helpful than this was the editorial aid he gave me when I was writing under pressure of a thesis deadline.)

Secondly, Burrhus was a solitary worker (*Schedules of Reinforcmement* is the principal exception) and a very cautious one. He didn't describe his experiments in advance of their execution; he never responded hastily to a challenging question (sometimes the answer was delayed for years); and he didn't announce a finding until he felt it was secure. He was not the kind to discuss his hopes or plans or half-analyzed data around the laboratory coffeepot, at the dinner table, or with a drink in hand at some convention. Such prudence may win respect, but is unlikely to initiate joint enterprise.

There is still another reason for our lack of important interaction in the twenties. In spite of his genius in experimental research, Burrhus Skinner was primarily a systematist, even then, and I was essentially a teacher. While he was doing the spadework for his paper on the reflex, I was translating mentalistic terms into stimulus-response and peddling the result to college undergraduates as a kind of ready-to-wear behaviorism. Nothing I ever got from him helped me much in composing lectures, and he got even less from me with which to further his ends. He was a producer of system; I was a promoter, and he had nothing yet ready for promotion.

I was, however, fully aware of his talent and I never expected less than a brilliant future for him. I was impressed by his study, reported at Colloquium, of eating behavior in the rat, although I did not recognize that *responses* could have replaced *pellets* on the y-axes of his plots. Later on, in the years between 1931 and 1938, I read his other papers as they came along, and even bought a *Skinner Box* (for $45.00), but I saw his contributions as mainly methodological. It was not until the summer of '38, when I began to read my copy of *The Behavior of Organisms,* that I finally saw what had been happening. Then, at last, I had something systematically exciting to give my classes, and a new phase of my own career began. But that is another story.

The changes in experimental-theoretical psychology during the past forty years have been far greater than commonly recognized by younger workers in our field. Within this period, for example, "schools" of psychology have passed quietly into history; "theories of learning" have come and gone (or should have); the laboratory experiment has replaced the polemic; and a self-supporting science of individual human behavior has emerged, along with an increasingly effective *praxis.* These changes are closely related to the fact that, within this same time span, a field of research called "learning" was crudely circumscribed, integrated, and extended.

In 1926, we could study, each in its own special chapter, textbook, or course: (a) memory and forgetting, (b) transfer of training, (c) maze learning, problem-box solution, and delayed-reaction capacity, (d) ball-tossing, dart-throwing, and Morse-code mastery, (e) concept formation, (f) language development, and (g) the newly-reported conditioned reflex. (Koehler's *Mentality of Apes* had barely reached us, hence "insight" and the *Umweg* method were not part of our usual offerings.) Each of these topics was uncontaminated by contact with the others, and any meaningful relation found between them was largely accidental and sometimes a source of worry.

In 1926, the most popular instruments for the laboratory study of behavior change were the maze and the memory drum; the principal measures of such change were those of *time and errors per trial;* the subjects were mainly white rats and college students. Great interest was shown in "learning curves," based on group data, and in the validity of certain "laws" of memory and habit formation (e.g., *frequency, recency, primacy, vividness, effect, completeness of response,* and *contiguity*). *Forgetting* was of some interest, especially in the case of nonsense syllables and other verbal material, and a few procedures had been suggested for the breaking of "bad habits"; but the concept of *extinction* was still around the corner, and that of behavior *maintenance* was ten years' distant or more. Pavlov's system was unknown, and so were Guthrie's views on the Russian's basic paradigm. Hull and his pupils were still several years away from taking the concept into the laboratory.

In 1926, learning research was hypothesis oriented, crude in design, and instrumentally primitive. The picture of a psychologist was that of a man in a laboratory coat, pencil in one hand and stopwatch in the other, seated behind a screen through a hole in which he could observe a white rat on an elevated maze. Replications of research were rarely attempted and even more rarely achieved. Results were not trusted, sometimes not even by the investigator himself. Orderliness of change in an individual organism's behavior, except in the case of sensory studies, was unheard-of.

This was the situation in 1926, as well as I can remember. It is not the situation that exists today in the great centers of advanced psychological study. Memory, maze-learning, conditioning, and concept formation are now to be found within the same universe of scientific discourse and are now part of a theoretical formulation that also has within it a place for such traditionally unrelated elements as those of motivation, instinct, emotion, sensation, perception, and imagery. The field of "learning," as distinct from the field of psychology itself, is increasingly difficult to identify, and the word *learning* itself is passing from our technical vocabulary. Problems of long-term behavior maintenance have taken the play from those of simple acquisition and elimination.

The maze and the memory drum are ticketed for the *omnium gatherum* of psychological relics; the old "laws" of memory and learning have lost their allure; and the search for "the learning curve" no longer attracts volunteers. But smooth curves of behavioral change are now common, for the individual as well as the group; successful replication of experimental findings is the rule; and the day approaches, perhaps, when the application of mathematics to the description of human and animal behavior will be systematically meaningful.

Where and when did the movement begin which made the difference between 1926 and now? Historians will give better answers to this question than I could possibly provide. But I shall trade upon my own before-and-after status to suggest that it all started at Harvard University, during the late twenties and early thirties, in the experimental and theoretical labors of Burrhus Frederic Skinner.

As for my part in all this, I would now like to quote the inscription in my dogeared copy of *The Behavior of Organisms: To Fred Keller—for friendship and faith when they were most needed—Burrhus.*

Notes

1. Here they are: Herbert Barry, Jr.; Weston A. Bousfield; Edw. N. Brush; A. Hadley Cantril, Jr.; Merton E. Carver; Dwight W. Chapman; James D. Coronios; Harry R. DeSilva; Crawford Goldthwait; Albert J. Harris; Wm. A. Hunt; Paul E. Huston, Theodore F. Karwoski; Hyung Lin Kim; Donald W. McKinnon; Eugene F. McCarthy; Ross A. McFarland; Edw. Newbury; Kermit W. Oberlin; R. Nevitt Sanford; David Shakow; Muzafer Sherif; B. F. Skinner; Carl E. Smith; Wm. H. Stavsky; Chas. K. Trueblood; Wm. D. Turner; John Volkmann; and Robert W. White. (There were others whom I never saw, one whose name I cannot remember, and perhaps a couple I may have overlooked.)

2. B. F. Skinner was, and is, known to most of his friends as *Fred,* but I gradually adopted *Burrhus,* hoping, I suppose, to avoid confusion in small group conversation. The hope was not realized, but my habit persists.

3. I must also mention H. C. Gilhousen, already a Ph.D., from Tolman's laboratory, who was a research assistant and a tutor, but with us in spirit. A dedicated student of behavior and a talented commentator on the social scene, "Gil" was one of the bright spots in my last two graduate years, and our relationship still endures.

2

Early Reinforcement Theory at Columbia

A few years ago, on reading the draft of a paper on the growth of "operant conditioning" in our time, I decided that something should be written about Columbia University's contribution to this movement by someone who was actively involved. I had completed most of the following account when I realized that I was not the only person qualified to tell the story. In a chat with W. N. Schoenfeld at the Washington meeting of the A.P.A. in 1971, we agreed to write independent parallel descriptions of what we thought had happened during the time we were together on Morningside Heights. Other demands upon our time, however, kept the project from getting off the ground. What follows is my first chapter on the topic. It should help in the transition from the Skinner *Festschrift* paper to the studies of Morse-code learning that will follow.

If I were to pick one year, above all others, which marked a turning point in my career, it would be 1938. That was the year in which B. F. Skinner's *Behavior of Organisms* was published and the year I accepted an instructorship at Columbia College. These two events, for me, were importantly related. Without *The Behavior of Organisms* my contribution to Columbia's program of teaching and research would have added little that was not already there; and, without Columbia, the system of behavior outlined in *The B of O* could not have been optimally exploited.

My initial attempt to connect Columbia with reinforcement theory was something of a failure. At an evening meeting of the psychology staff, in the home of John Volkmann, I tried to tell the members present about the great new book I had been reading. The occasion was pleasant, my colleagues were cordial, and I embarked upon my task with enthusiasm. All went well for several minutes, until I got to Skinner's definition of the reflex as an observed correlation between a stimulus and a response. It was there that trouble began.

Professor Warden led off. He explained, in forthright terms, just what a reflex really was. His aggressive approach, his position of seniority, and his reputation as a comparative psychologist combined to leave me gulping and defenseless. What reply I might have mustered, I will never know. For, just in the nick of time, Professor Klineberg, as smooth and conciliatory as Warden was rough and unyielding, came to my assistance, modestly proposing a counter definition.

From that time on, the matter was out of my hands. I don't know what would have happened if I had reached the topic of *operant* behavior, which "does not seem to be elicited," but which may still be *reflex*. It's just as well that I never completed my review.

I went to Columbia in the post-depression period, after seven lean years at Colgate University without promotion or a raise in pay, and I brought my research equipment with me—a Skinner Box and a cumulative recorder.[1] With this much of a start, I hoped to find a place for some of the studies that were suggesting themselves as I perused *The B of O*. I had a lighter load of teaching than before, and my mouth watered when I visited Professor Warden's large domain on the second floor of Schermerhorn Extension.

Disappointment met my early efforts to find a place for animal research. Professor Warden advised me that all his space was needed for graduate-student projects. He even showed annoyance at my desire to work within his realm. "I thought you were interested in 'schools,' " he said. Professor Poffenberger, our Chairman, to whom I went for help, counselled patience; so I turned to other possibilities.

In late January of 1939, I took my apparatus home, to study the lever-pressing response in my 17-month-old daughter, under several conditions of reward with bits of chocolate. Within a two- to three-day period she provided me with cumulative records of conditioning, satiation, intermittent reinforcement, and extinction. I made slides from the curves I had collected, and showed them at some professional gathering (I can't remember where), but I never tried to publish. The study was dead, for me, before it was done. I had known in advance what would happen, that the child would behave like a rat! And so she did, except for one small difference. In extinction she held on to the bar of the lever and shook it, in little volleys of response. It even seemed a sign of weakness to have carried out the study, or to have thought that it was needed. It was like doubting evolution!

A chance for animal research came from an unexpected quarter, by way of a Barach Portable Oxygen Chamber and Clifford P. Seitz, on Schermerhorn's third floor, normally reserved for human studies. Seitz, in a pause between his dissertation and a job at Alabama, was skilled in low-oxygen technique, keen on methodology in general, and eager to collaborate. We set up my box and recorder in his tent and proceeded to investigate response rate in the white rat, at sea level and at a simulated altitude of 17,500 feet.

We completed one experiment, in which science gained little, but nearly lost me—at 14,000 feet, as I recall it, without an oxygen mask. We then embarked upon a second study, involving long-term oxygen deprivation and its effect upon extinction of response. This investigation came to an abrupt and untimely end when our oxygen supply ran out one night and most of our rats succumbed.

Not long after this, I found myself an unused room on the second floor, complete with a sound-resistant chamber which I didn't really need, and at the other end of the corridor from Professor Warden. (The latter had relented to the point of supplying me with water bottles, food, and Monelmetal cages for my experimental subjects.) I cleared away the debris from earlier occupancy, moved in my apparatus, and happily staked out my claim with a name card on the door. Now, for sure, research would be forthcoming.

Within the year that followed, I was able to find that two groups of rats, each taught to operate a lever for food under two schedules of reinforcement (food for each response and food at three-minute intervals), were equally resistant to extinction of the response, regardless of the *sequence* in which the two schedules had been used. This finding excited very little comment. Somewhat more impressive was my demonstration that (albino) rats could be trained to turn off a light with a bar-press if a minute of darkness followed the response. I began to talk of *light aversion* and tried, with the help of an undergraduate,[2] to show that certain *sounds,* like that of jingling keys, were aversive too, but our results were unstable and less convincing.

By 1940 I had built up my classroom defenses against a tougher breed of student than Colgate had provided; I had formed a few friendships with younger staff members and graduate assistants; and I had sponsored my first research for the Master's degree—an animal study by Herbert Hyman,[3] the scientific goal of which I can't remember. In addition, and more important, I had brought in my first doctoral dissertation—an experimental study of human *differentiation* by Matthew J. Murphy (working, not at Columbia, but New York University). Murphy, the friend of one of my former Colgate pupils,[4] who had come to N.Y.U. for graduate study, caught some of my enthusiasm for *The B of O.* Fired by Skinner's work with *force* of the bar-pressing response in rats, he undertook to check it out with human beings and a pinball machine, cleverly adapted to a nobler purpose than a game of chance. Thus it came about that the first "Columbia" extension of reinforcement thinking to the study of human skill was actually not Columbian in its setting.

Another, even more important, event for me in 1940 was *Gardner* Murphy's departure for a higher level post (long overdue) at City College. In addition to his other functions within our Department, Professor Murphy had taught the introductory course at Columbia College, a very popular offering in which John Volkmann, Otto Klineberg, and I had presided at discussion sections. When Gardner finally decided to leave, John and I were chosen to replace him as well as we could; John was to deal with sensory-physiological matters, and I with learning and motivation.

The pressure on us was very great. Gardner had been "a man for all seasons," whereas John was currently fixated on psychophysical judgment and I on the Skinner Box. How could we possibly fill the shoes of a man who ranged from Pavlov to Piaget to *Middletown Revisited* within a period of fifty minutes; who worked from a few scribbled notes on the back of an envelope, but gave a polished performance (like a chapter in an interesting book) that ended within seconds of the classroom bell; who could sell three competing psychotherapeutic views to scores of sophomores in three successive lectures; and who, with no apparent histrionics, stirred his audience on occasion to a state approaching tears?[5] Psychology 1-2 at Columbia College, after Gardner Murphy, was never quite the same.

Association with this new first course meant several things to me. Most importantly it opened the door to teaching reinforcement theory at the undergraduate level. Little by little, as I saw their connection with the topics assigned to me, I introduced the concepts of operant conditioning, extinction, generalization, and discrimination within my portion of the course. I found that students, whether bent towards art or science, enjoyed a systematic treatment of behavior and quickly rose to the bait of a biological approach. Volkmann saw this too but, with a more classical and sensory bias, restrained me from excesses, and we began to see modes of accommodation to each other's major themes. What would have happened had we stayed together is an interesting question.[6]

Gardner Murphy's departure left an opening for a new man on our staff. At a meeting called to consider the matter, it became apparent that suggestions for his replacement would be welcomed from Volkmann and me, in spite of our instructor status. It didn't take us long to come up with names and, although we had but one apiece to place before the group, each of us approved the other's choice. We both picked men whose work was well known to us and we both picked Harvard products. John's choice was S. S. (Smitty) Stevens, a Ph.D. of '53 who had stayed on in Emerson Hall as an instructor and was currently one step higher, with a 'promising' future. I picked, guess who, the author of the *Behavior of Organisms,* a freshly promoted associate professor at the University of Minnesota, who would obviously be glad to return to the East after such a period of "exile" (my term, not his)—namely, B. F. (Fred) Skinner.

I do not recall in detail the discussions we had of this problem or all the arguments with which Volkmann and I defended our candidates. I talked of Skinner's record and his virtues. I argued, quite correctly, that he wasn't in love with the rat *per se.* I said that his major interest at that time was verbal behavior, on which he had been working since 1934, and that he would in no case pose a threat to Professor Warden or his laboratory space. Volkmann's brief was masterfully assembled and eloquently presented, but the minutiae elude me now.

Neither of us was fated to prevail. Many considerations, some of them irrelevant,[7] dictated the final choice, which could hardly be called a bad one—that of Clarence H. (Clancy) Graham, then at Brown. Although pro-Skinner and pro-Stevens, we could *not* be anti-Graham. In this way the matter was happily resolved.

Murphy's leaving had still another outcome: an office for me on the second floor, just two doors away from my laboratory room. With Volkmann's help, the two rooms were soon electrically connected, and it was possible to gather data and control experimental changes while working at my desk or performing other duties. The value of my association with graduate-school facilities, students, and colleagues began to be apparent, and I was soon caught up in a number of collaborative ventures.

The light-aversion study suggested some of these. For example, Horace Corbin,[8] a graduate assistant working under Volkmann, joined me in a study of the way in which a time discrimination is acquired. Our 'rats' were graduate students, working with the animal apparatus and in my sound-resistant chamber, with the following instructions (delivered orally and posted on the chamber wall):

> Your task in this experiment is to keep the light out in this room as much of the time as possible, with the least number of bar-pressings. (Only the depression of the lever, in the box before you, will turn off the light.)
>
> Your score on this performance will be based on the amount of time that the light is on when it could be off (the shorter this time the better), but it will also depend on the number of pressings you make (the fewer the better).

Then the student was left alone until we turned off his light from my office and the experiment began. For five trials in a row the light went off for 30 seconds as soon as the bar was pressed. (By the fifth response to the light, his reaction time was usually very short.) At this point we changed the rules. No matter how many times the student pressed the bar when the light came on, he couldn't turn it off until 15 seconds had elapsed. Any response within that period was without effect, serving only to lower the student's score.

What happened under these conditions was an orderly decrease in the number of presses during successive 15-second periods of light, until the time discrimination was set up—when the bar presses occurred just before, or just after, 15 seconds had gone by. One of our subjects, however, stopped responding entirely during the experimental period.[9] We found her in the dark, having turned off the light at the socket switch above her in order to improve her score.

In the same experiment, following this time discrimination and while the subject was still at work within his experimental cubicle, we introduced another change in rules. Our student no longer had to wait 15 seconds before his response would be effective; he had only to press the bar *twice* to get the light off. We moved, that is, from a *fixed-interval* schedule of reinforcement to one of *fixed ratio* (a ratio of two responses per reinforcement). This was done without the subject's knowledge, just as we had moved earlier from consecutive reinforcements to fixed-interval.

The effect of this upon each subject was initially the same. After the first occasion on which two responses were needed to turn off the light, the subject on the *next* occasion always took a longer time to make the first bar-press of the pair. He said to himself, in effect, "I must have responded too soon; I'll wait a little longer this time." On the third occasion, the subject's first reaction might be even more delayed. One student stretched this time to more than 40 minutes. Others solved the problem without trouble, but in a manner which suggested that they had first to make their two responses *in close succession* before they caught on to the contingency in effect. This led us to some speculation about the meaning of "response." Could two responses come to function just like one? This question bothered us later on from time to time.

The light-aversion finding set off several other studies within a year or two. In one of these Volkmann was the principal contributor. Rats had shown a tendency, upon turning off the light, to hold the bar in the 'down' position or to make several 'extra' responses within the minute of darkness. Both behaviors seemed related to the brightness of the light employed, but got in each other's way as measures of the strength of the response. If the animal held the bar down, he couldn't make the extras, and *vice versa.* Volkmann designed a three-element lever, one bar of which rotated out of the animal's response chamber when he pressed, letting another drop into place from above. *Holding* was made impossible, but *extras* were permitted. I don't recall that we ever found more lawfulness of extras as a result of this new lever, but Ralph Hefferline[10] used it later to good effect in his classic studies of avoidance.

Another collaborator at this time was Kermit Oberlin, a friend from graduate-school days, who was then at Delaware. Oberlin helped to develop a simple shuttle-box procedure for classroom demonstrations of light-escape and light-avoidance (we called it "light-dark preference"). It was a crude but effective device that any undergraduate department could afford, although I have never heard of any that did. We found that both escape behavior (running from the lighted end of the box) and avoidance (staying in the darkened end) could be easily established and maintained.[11]

By 1941 even undergraduates were working in our little laboratory. One young man, named Robert Jastrow, who took our elementary course while still a freshman, was especially promising, although 'left-handed' with equipment. I encouraged him to take more mathematics, as a desirable tool for further study in our field. He followed my advice, but fell in love with the 'tool' and veered away to physics and, ultimately, a distinguished career.[12] None of us ever untangled the electrical circuits that he left behind in my little laboratory room.

In the same year (1941), probably at Volkmann's suggestion, I was invited to report on my "researches" at a December meeting of the PRT (Psychological Round Table) in Northampton, Massachusetts. This group of self-styled "experimenting" psychologists was a kind of counter-attraction in the East to the *Society of Experimental Psychologists* which

Titchener had founded. I was very proud to attend, even as one whose age exceeded the PRT limit of 40 and marked him as finished. I went with Volkmann and Youtz,[13] who were members, and in the main I had a pleasant time, marred only by a cruel (even if merited) comment from a former friend of graduate-school days, to the effect that "everyone knew" where I got *my* ideas. I am very happy to say that most of my "friends" since then have been less direct in asserting my intellectual dependence!

The important event of this trip, however, took place on the wintry Sunday morning of our return, December 7th. We had a radio in our car and it brought us news of the Japanese attack on Pearl Harbor. This meant for each of us changes that we could not then foresee, but which would greatly affect our lives for several years thereafter. Volkmann would be on "special research" at Harvard; Youtz would be an Air Force officer (the first or second in his graduating class, I think) and researcher; and I would have a training project at Camp Crowder, in Missouri, with the Signal Corps. World War II, like World War I, was 'popular' in our country, and everyone took part who could.

Notes

1. The Skinner Box was early Gerbrands, described in *The Behavior of Organisms;* and the cumulative recorder, made by a friend in the Physics Department (a brother-in-law of the psychologist Douglas Ellson), was built from a Harvard kymograph drum, a Telechron clock motor, two Boston gears, a single ball-bearing, four supporting parts, a two-foot brass rod, a piece of silk thread, and a Bristol pen. My yearly research fund at Colgate was $25, which encouraged economies.

2. Edward P. Bindrim.

3. Herbert H. Hyman, later a Professor of Sociology at Columbia, was never really devoted to the white rat, to individual psychology, or to reinforcement theory, but did quite well for himself in spite of such obvious handicaps.

4. F. L. Reinwald, now Professor of Psychology at Colgate, carried out two predoctoral studies, both unpublished, which strongly suggested the failure of Pavlov's basic procedure when applied to the motor, rather than the glandular, responses of rats and dogs. Like Murphy, he had considerable skill in building apparatus, and provided me with a recording element that I needed badly in my early efforts at Columbia.

5. His lecture on Alfred Adler was one of many works of art. I had listened to Adler in Vienna several times, but he never equalled Murphy in emotional appeal. When Gardner traced Lord Byron's deeds, even the swimming of the Hellespont, to a congenital clubfoot and a mother's reference, overheard, to "that lame brat," Adler came alive in a very special way.

6. In 1946, Volkmann left us for Mt. Holyoke where he has had an illustrious career of teaching and research. A dedicated scientist and a highly productive teacher, he and his colleagues have made Mt. Holyoke's name distinguished as a psychological center.

7. One such issue, which I have heard in similar meetings since, concerned the "personal" qualities of our nominees. "Is it true he's hard to get along with?" "Do you think he'd make a good member of our family?" The implication being that the man in question *is,* and *wouldn't.* Our answer was another question: "Is it ability that you want, or amiability?"

8. Another hard-working member of the Mt. Holyoke group, Corbin joined the staff in 1947, after military service.

9. It seems to me that this subject was Alberta (Steinman) Gilinsky, another Volkmann protegee, who was just beginning graduate study. If so, it was not the last occasion on which she showed resourcefulness and initiative!

10. Hefferline, R. F. An experimental study of avoidance. *Genetic Psychology Monographs,* 1950, *42,* 231-334.

11. Keller, F. S. and Oberlin, K. W. A simple technique for measuring light-dark preference in the white rat. *Journal of Genetic Psychology, 61,* 163-166.

12. Robert Jastrow is currently at Columbia, an Adjunct Professor of Geology, in addition to his other scientific posts.

13. Richard E. P. Youtz, Professor of Psychology at Barnard College, had come back to Columbia from Oberlin College in 1940. The Youtzes, Volkmanns, and Kellers were friends and neighbors on Morningside Drive.

3

Dots and Dashes

What was to have been the second chapter of my account of Columbia's early contributions to the experimental analysis of behavior was reported in part at the Third Annual Southern California Conference on Behavior Modification, at Los Angeles, on October 8th, 1971, under the title of *Snapshots from the Album of a Behavior Modifier.* Some of that address is repeated here, along with sections of the chapter not previously reported. (These latter sections are in brackets.)

In the early years of this century I was a telegraph messenger boy in a Western New York State town. I wore a blue uniform and a visored cap, and I rode a bicycle six days a week in the speedy discharge of my duties. I delivered the news of births and deaths, of lovers' trysts and baseball games, of disasters at sea and on land, of state and national elections, stock market ups and downs, and business dealings of various kinds. People generally viewed my coming with interest, alarm, or hope, and they usually reinforced me with ten-cent pieces for my service. Along with Mr. Merker, the office manager, and Mr. Thompson, our regular operator, I was the town's main point of contact with the outside world. Long-distance telephone calls had not yet reached practicality; the telegrapher at the Erie Railroad station had special duties connected with transportation; and the only other communication from afar was by way of a beeping tone from Arlington, Virginia, by which our local jeweler set his clocks.

The glamor of this position and the lure of a secret language encouraged me to learn the telegraphic code. Mr. Merker rigged up a key and sounder on my back-room desk, gave me a list of Morse-code signals, and wished me Godspeed. Between my telegram deliveries, and sometimes when off duty, I sat at my desk and tapped my key, or I listened to the clatter of incoming messages and the fainter sounds of a relay clicking intermittently in one corner of our office. Once in awhile, to my great satisfaction, Mr. Merker, who had been crippled when a boy, would wheel his chair out to my desk and give me slow-speed lessons in receiving, or listen to my own transmissions. (Mr. Thompson wouldn't help me and pretended to be sorry for anyone so foolish as to pick 'brass pounding' for a trade.) My progress was slow, but I endured. Within a few months I had learned to send all the signals, to recognize some office call signs, and catch an occasional short word from an incoming message.

My apprenticeship was interrupted when my family moved to another town, but I soon renewed my efforts, under a new manager and with a new operator to counsel me in personal and professional matters. Within a year I was employed as a full-time telegrapher, at $45 a month, on the afternoon and evening shift.

This work ended during World War I when I enlisted in the Army with a friend of mine to serve, not in the Signal Corps where I belonged, but in the Field Artillery. This interruption was important, since it led me back to formal education and, finally, to a different way of life. Thereafter I plied my trade only on a part-time basis, to support my studies. Finally, I gave it up entirely, with considerable regret. But I knew, like Willie Grogan in Saroyan's *Human Comedy,* that the days of commercial telegraphy were numbered. I thought I'd never have occasion to use the skill again.

******

At the start of World War II, however, my interest was drawn once more to Morse-code matters. A need was felt for greater speed in the training of radio operators for military function. The supply of radio *hams* was seen to be inadequate, even if they were all called up, and the time required for beginners to attain a minimal skill was causing great concern. The highly advertised *walkie-talkie* had not replaced the dot-and-dash procedure.

Ever since the days of Bryan and Harter, with their classic work on Morse-code learning, psychologists have treated this field of training as especially their own. In times of unusual need, as in World Wars I and II, they come from every quarter to attack the problem. I was no exception. I heard the siren call with special clarity because of my earlier occupation, and I hurried to apply the rules of reinforcement theory to the problem.

To use Morse code, as everyone knows, is *to send* or *to receive* a set of auditory signals—patterns of clicks in American Morse, or of long and short tones in the International code. The difficulty that students have in mastering the code is not in learning to send, but to receive—to write, print, or type the appropriate letter or digit in quick response to the auditory pattern. Signals get mixed up with one another when they come in fast succession. Therefore, it is on receiving that researchers usually focus their attention.

The problem for me resolved itself into one of *stimulus discrimination,* and the white rat in the Skinner Box was my experimental model. I decided that this little animal, pressing a lever whenever a tone was sounded in his chamber, was really a radio operator, working with a one-signal code and a very simple "copying" response, the bar-press. Except, perhaps, for one important difference: if the rat performs this function, he typically gets a pellet of food for his trouble, whereas the operator's reward is not so easily observed.

An attack was launched on various fronts. Students, staff, and friends joined me in one phase of the campaign or another. An undergraduate seminar tracked down reports on code research and training methods; colleagues and assistants assembled crude equipment for producing signals—auditory, visual, even tactual; and visits were made to nearby training centers, both military and civilian. Formal and informal experiments were conducted. Code was taught in classrooms, in my office, and at several dining-room tables on Morningside Drive.

Early in this period, a "code-voice" method of teaching was developed. I would sound a signal with my key; about three seconds later I would announce the signal's name—the letter or the digit; in the time between the signal and the voice, my pupil would try to print the appropriate character on a sheet of paper. If he succeeded, the announcement presumably rein-

28

forced his action; if he failed, it told him of his error. All of the basic 36 signals were used, right from the start of training. They were sent in 'runs' of 100 signals each; and we kept a record of the errors made. Progress curves could be constructed from these records.[1]

The aim of this procedure was threefold: (1) to encourage the student to react to every signal of the code when it was sent; (2) to provide immediate reinforcement for each correct response; and (3) to determine the nature of every error made. The procedure permitted the individual student to move to a higher level of training as soon as he showed that he was ready to do so.

[One of my earliest subjects, Richard Youtz, gave me nothing very useful with which to make a curve. On his first practice runs his error scores were large, and typical, but on the next evening, at his second training session, he made no errors at all. For a very good reason: on one side of each of 36 cards he had pictured a basic signal, in dot-dash form; on the other he had written the matching letter or digit; at spare moments throughout the day, he would look at the dots and dashes, *whistle* their pattern, and guess at the name before checking. He taught me more than did those students who obeyed the rules.

Another of my code beginners was Spaulding Rogers, a Volkmann Ph.D. in '41 and a teacher at Hofstra College.[2] He too learned the code with ease, and took an active part in our endeavor. He went with me on visits to see how code was taught at Fort Monmouth, New Jersey, and at other training centers, and he suggested several features of the method that we finally adopted. An important one of these was the code-receiving form which permitted a rapid assessment, by the student as well as his teacher, of the kind and number of errors made on every training run.]

Along with the attempt to develop a method of our own for teaching code, we tried to find out the official military method. Security measures sometimes blocked us. For example, we tried to get a copy of the training manual that described the Signal Corps procedure, of which we had only secondhand accounts. We were told that it was "classified." Our annoyance was intense and we were quite persistent, but the Corps stood firm. If it hadn't been for Robert Taubman,[3] my graduate assistant, who borrowed the manual from the Columbia library, we might never have obtained it,

As the code-voice procedure took shape and was found to be effective, the news was passed along. Would-be experimental subjects came to us from the college staff and student body, seeking to learn the rudiments of code before their military service. A code school was suggested, approved by the Dean, and finally set up in our Department. Two points of credit were offered per semester for a daily hour of practice and a final speed of at least 10 words per minute. Now we could make group studies, and each member of the class was committed to take part.

One of our pupils in this course had heard that code signals were really *Gestalten*—little German entities of sound that should never be broken down into dots and dashes if their optimal reception was ever to be achieved. He volunteered to learn the code in a way that seemed consistent with this view. Instead of visualizing a dot and dash or murmuring *di-dah* between the signal and his printing of the letter *A*, for example, he would react to the little pattern as fast as he could when it was sent, and then await the news of success or failure. That is, he would not permit himself to analyze the signal, as beginners usually do, before he wrote the letter or the digit. He used this method and, in spite of slower progress than we had ever seen by any student, in time he might have learned the code—I cannot say. His Draft Board turned him down, however, as unfit for military service, which brought the experiment to an end.

[Many of our studies in those days were never published, and could not have been, in the stage at which we dropped them. Yet they gave us what we wanted, providing us with further leads or keeping us from barking up wrong trees. In one experiment, for example, we sought to teach the code by a procedure, often urged upon us, of simultaneous stimulation. A tonal dot and dash came through the student's ear-phones; its visual counterpart came from a blinking light on the table just before him; and, on the back of his hand, a vibrator told a similar story. Each stimulus pattern by itself can serve as a Morse-code signal; should they not, in combination, have a greater impact? The answer that we got was *No*. Our subjects reported selective attention to the sound, the light, or the vibration, and their rate of learning did not seem to be affected in one way or the other. If anything, the multiple stimulation was distracting. We discontinued our attempts in this direction.

Throughout this busy period, the code-school prospered, with as many as 60 students in a class. They came mainly from the College, but occasionally a graduate student would join the group, or even a faculty member. Two of the latter remained to act as instructors before their call to military service.[4] One young man, a psychology instructor at Barnard College,[5] mastered basic code in a way that has some bearing on experimental findings in the field of verbal learning. He was individually taught by the code-voide method, with 50 signals in each practice run. All the letters and digits were represented in each run and *always in the same order*. Thus, *O* would be followed by *A, A* by *2, 2* by *S, S* by *V,* and so on, in every practice run. The only difference between successive runs was in the starting signal—Run 1 might start with *O,* for example, Run 2 would start with *A,* Run 3 with *2,* and so on.

At the point where this student made a run without any errors, the experiment was stopped and he was asked if he had noticed anything unusual about the sequence of signals in each run. "Only one thing," he answered, "I think the O was always followed by an A." An interesting question was thereby raised, but not pursued, concerning the role of "unnoticed" prior stimuli in paired-associate studies—a problem not without precedent in the literature on learning.[6]]

Our efforts reached their practical peak within a military setting. A small research-and-development group was established at one of the training centers of the Signal Corps.[7] In this environment, basic research dropped off in volume and we coped with problems that we hadn't met before. We learned that sanction from above doesn't guarantee cooperation from below. We found that public relations are sometimes more important than incontrovertible data in getting changes made. We discovered that a vested interest in an old procedure can block acceptance of any new departure; and that nothing can be assured to last when one is gone, unless it is in a training manual!

Control groups, in this period, suddenly disappeared or were exposed to experimental group procedures; 'typical' progress records from earlier comparison groups of trainees were found to be less than typical when examined closely; critical training conditions were occasionally disrupted without warning; and other minor indignities were sometimes suffered at the hands of those we sought to help with our endeavors.

In the main, however, the project was successful. Our presence came to be accepted, our data to be respected, and our positive contributions found their place within the training system. More and more we felt like members of the family. More and more the camp itself took on the aspect of a university. Our commandant became its president, with brigadiers and colonels as vice-presidents and deans. We had associate deans, assistant deans, and chairmen. Without the uniform, the military manner, and the disagreeable habit of early rising, and with a little grass, trees and ivy, we might occasionally have wondered where we were.

Differences of course existed. It was a university with limited aims and with the burden of accountability for its teachings and researches. Its purposes were stated in terms of human action, and the test of its excellence was expressed in the form of human survival. Its students were conscripted, in the main, and they majored in those areas where the need was greatest. If they failed to pass their courses with an A, they were sent to other departments or institutions. Combat communication has no place for C-grade students.

Especially different was the teaching system. The professors and instructors—the captains and lieutenants—seldom lectured. Their role was one of overseeing, planning, and providing motivation, in accord with dictates from above. It was the noncommissioned officer, the sergeant or the corporal, sometimes the first-class private, who had the task of guiding, clarifying, demonstrating, testing, grading, and the like. These men were often graduates of earlier classes in the school, sometimes back from active duty, and were intimately aware of the pupils' needs and problems. They gave individual attention, immediate reinforcement and, by virtue of their function in some courses, they enabled students to advance when they were ready.

All this, of course, was more or less irrelevant to university instruction! What I took back to the campus, when our work was done, was something else entirely: the simple faith that reinforcement theory could be applied successfully in the field of Morse-code skill, and possibly to other skills as well. This strengthened my belief that a thorough treatment of the viewpoint was suitable at the college level. It was only a step from there to the notion of laboratory sessions in which, by using the albino rat, most of our basic laws could be seen in action by beginners.

Notes

1. The paper describing this procedure was the first of a number that resulted from our efforts: Studies in International Morse Code. I. A new method of teaching code reception. J. Appl. Psychol., 1943, 27, 504-509.

2. Professor Rogers, now at Rockford College (Illinois), went on from Hofstra and Columbia to run a code school at Camp Edwards, Massachusetts, from which he was later drawn to serve with "Intelligence" in London (where he shared quarters, as I recall it, with Ralph Ingersoll of the short-lived New York daily paper, PM). Without Spaulding's aid and lively wit, our code work would have been less effective and much less animated.

3. Dr. Robert E. Taubman, now a psychiatrist in Eugene, Oregon, did early work on code-related problems at Columbia and was my first collaborator in the field (in a study of errors made in code receiving by beginners). He was later assigned to work with me at Camp Crowder (now Fort Crowder), on an N.D.R.C. project for the Signal Corps. He received his Ph.D. in 1948 at Columbia, for a study of auditory number.

4. Wilbur M. Frohock, the French scholar, who later went on to Harvard, brushed up on his code and helped us while awaiting active duty in the Navy. Charles Frankel, now a Professor of Philosophy and Public Affairs at Columbia, learned the code quickly and reached a relatively high level of proficiency, but went on to language school and more important Naval functions than those of a radio operator.

5. Thomas G. Andrews, late Professor of Psychology and Head of the Department at the University of Maryland.

6. See Thorndike's argument for a principle of "belongingness," in his *Psychology of Wants, Interests, and Attitudes,* New York: Appleton Century, 1935.

4

Stimulus Discrimination and Morse-Code Learning

Early in 1953 I was asked to speak to the New York Academy of Sciences on our Morse-code studies. With World War II behind us, code researches were falling off in number and in the interest they aroused. This was an excellent opportunity to draw together the researches in which I had taken part and to place them in historical perspective, thereby bringing to a close (or so I thought) my interest in the matter. I accepted the invitation with alacrity and went to work immediately on the paper. I was helped in getting under way by my colleague, friend, and former pupil, the late William W. Cumming, who drew my attention to the item on auditory Morse published in *Scientific American.*

This paper is reprinted from the *Transactions* of the New York Academy of Sciences (1953, Series II, Vol. 15, 195-203). Copyright 1953 by the New York Academy of Sciences. It is reprinted with permission from *Transactions.*

The January issue of this year's *Scientific American* contains an excerpt from the same journal for January, 1853. It is to the effect that the operators of the Buffalo-Milwaukee telegraph, "working under Morse's patent," have stopped using the visual signals made by Morse's instrument and pay attention only to the *auditory* cues that the signals provide as they are recorded. "The different sounds are made by the striking of the pen lever upon a piece of brass: thus, three raps in rapid succession are made for the letter 'A,' two raps, an interval, and then two raps more are made for 'B,' and so forth."

This item nearly led me to write a letter to the editor, for two reasons: These operators were not the first to copy code by ear; and they were apparently using the wrong code!

Samuel Morse designed his famous telegraph to record *visual,* rather than auditory, code, but he probably recognized, as early as 1835 or 1836, that each code signal had its own distinctive pattern of sound, and he made this clear in the patent specifications drawn up in 1837-38.[9] Moreover, he had himself seen his recorder used as a "sounder" at least six years prior to 1853. He describes his experience in detail:

"The time of the incident was soon after the line was extended from Philadelphia to Washington, having a way station at Wilmington, Delaware. The Washington office was in the old post-office, in the room above it. I was in the operating room. The instruments were for a moment silent. I was standing at some distance near the fire-place conversing with Mr. Washington, the operator, who was by my side. Presently one of the instruments commenced writing and Mr. Washington listened and smiled. I asked him why he smiled. 'Oh!' said he, 'That is Zantzinger of the Philadelphia office, but he is operating from Wilmington.' 'How do you know that?' 'Oh! I know his touch, but I must ask him why he is in Wilmington.' He then went to the instrument and telegraphed to Zantzinger at Wilmington, and the reply was that he had been sent from Philadelphia to regulate the relay magnet for the Wilmington operator, who was inexerienced in operating.

"I give this instance not because it was the *first,* but because it is the one I had specially treasured in my memory and frequently related as illustrative of the practicality of reading by *sound* as well as by the written record. This must have occurred about the year 1846."[9]

As for the second point, the *Scientific American* names the signal for "A" as "three raps," and for "B," "two raps, an interval, and . . . two raps more." Yet the code to which these signals belonged was presumably out of date by 1853.

The first Morse code, invented by Morse in 1832, was composed of ten signals. These signals represented the ten digits. Morse pictured them as

Figure 1. Three Morse Codes

Character	Morse's Code No. 2	Morse's Code No. 3 (American Morse)	International Morse
A	• • •	• —	• —
B	• • • •	— • • •	— • • •
C	• • •	• • •	— • — •
D	• • • •	— • •	— • •
E	•	•	•
F	• • • •	• — •	• • — •
G	• • •	— — •	— — •
H	• • • •	• • • •	• • • •
I	• — •	• •	• •
J	• • •	— • — •	• — — —
K	— • —	— • —	— • —
L	—	—	• — • •
M	— • •	— —	— —
N	— •	— •	— •
O	• •	• •	— — —
P	• • • • •	• • • • •	• — — •
Q	• • — •	• • — •	— — • —
R	• •	• • •	• — •
S	• — •	• • •	• • •
T	— — •	—	—
U	• — —	• • —	• • —
V	—	• • • —	• • • —
W	• • —	— —	• — —
X	— —	• — • •	— • • —
Y	• —	• • • •	— • — —
Z	• — •	• • • •	— — • •
1		• — •	• — — — —
2		• • — • •	• • — — —
3		• • • — •	• • • — —
4		• • • • —	• • • • —
5	?	— — —	• • • • •
6		• • • • • •	— • • • •
7		— — • •	— — • • •
8		— • • • •	— — — • •
9		— • • —	— — — — •
0		——	— — — — —

dots and spaces between dots. Thus, the numbers 1, 2, 3, 4, and 5 were represented by one, two, three, four, and five dots, respectively, with each sequence followed by a pause that was perceptibly greater than the intra-signal space between dots. Six, 7, 8, 9, and 0 were also indicated by one to five dots, but the pause after each string was two-thirds again as large as that which followed each of the first five-digit signals.

Originally, Morse had intended to represent 6, 7, 8, 9, and 0 by six, seven, eight, nine, and ten dots. He tells us, however, that "a few minutes' reflection showed that after *five* dots or points the number of dots became inconveniently numerous in indicating the larger digits."[11] This interesting 'reflection' probably stemmed from Morse's failure to judge, correctly, at a single glance, the larger number of dots. This you can easily see for yourself:

· · · · · ·   · · · · · · ·   · · · · · · · ·   · · · · · · · · ·

· · · · · · · · · ·

Psychologists know that Morse's failure was not without precedent. Charles Bonnet, the Swiss naturalist and philosopher, had argued, back in 1760, that the mind could have no clear impression of more than a very limited number of objects (he said *six*) at one time. Psychologists may also note that Morse anticipated the observations of Sir William Hamilton, who threw marbles on the floor and found it "difficult to view at once more than six, or seven at most, without confusion." They remember, too, that Jevons, the logician, tossed beans into a little round box and found "absolute freedom from error in the numbers 3 and 4," but failed to judge the number 5 correctly in five per cent of the cases. It is clear to all of us today that Morse was making contact with the "span of attention" problem.[20]

In a very modern setting, Morse's observation has been paralleled almost exactly in part of a study' by Saltzman and Garner[12] at Johns Hopkins about five years ago. These investigators showed subjects from one to ten visual dots, in a straight line, and asked them to judge the number at each showing. They found that, with increasing dot number, there was a decrease in the accuracy of the reports. Moreover, the time required to report increased as the number of dots increased, even for numbers below the mystic five or six. Morse's "reflection" seems quite up to date!

The first Morse code was cryptographic. There were numbers for all of the letters and many of the words of the English language. Morse spent many hours in building a "telegraphic dictionary" to be used in coding and de-coding messages. These hours were wasted. His dictionary was barely completed when he decided to use an "alphabetic" code, in which each letter had its own signal. This second Morse code is shown in Figure 1.

It was probably introduced in 1838, and it is the code to which the *Scientific American* referred in its 1853 item. It was composed of the now conventional dots and dashes, and occasionally employed a special intra-signal space. This space can be seen in the signals for *B, C, D, F, G,* and *R.* You will note, too, that the signals for *G, I,* and *S* also did service for *J, Y,* and *Z.* Morse was a frugal man, or afraid that too many signals would reduce the appeal of his code!

But Code No. 2 had a short life. Within four years, Morse arrived at his third and final offering. This code followed upon a trip to a printing office where Morse determined the amount of type on hand for each letter in the compositor's case. This was done for the express purpose of relating the 'size' of the signal to the frequency of its usage.

Code No. 3 was employed in transmitting the famous message (*What hath God wrought!*) from Washington to Baltimore and back again on May 24th, 1844. It is the code that we now call "American Morse." It is also the code that should have been well known to the telegraph operators on the Buffalo-Milwaukee wire nine years later! It is here shown in Figure 1. This is the code that you may still hear occasionally in country railroad stations or on the broadcasts of baseball games.

Morse, in making up his first code, apparently recognized an important discriminative problem when he noted that visual dots became "inconveniently numerous" when they exceeded five. We have also given him credit for having anticipated the use of auditory rather than visual signals in transmitting the code. It does *not* appear, however, that he was ever aware of some of the discriminative problems raised for those whose task it would be, in later years, to receive the code *by ear.* His third code, although quite well suited for the work ahead, was nevertheless defective in one or two respects.

The first and least important fault had to do with those dot signals that contained an extra internal space. That is, the signals for *C, O, R, Y,* and *Z* in Figure 1. Careful spacing of these signals, and of their component dots, was required, if certain words were to be copied without error. For example:

P   I   E   R   C   E
. . . .

This difficulty, which came in with the hand-sending of the signals, was seldom very great, however, and today is virtually nonexistent. *International* Morse code, which replaced these signals by longer ones, composed of dots, dashes, and small spaces only, is now almost universally employed in radiotelegraphy.

The second defect in the third code, American Morse, was rooted mainly in five signals: *6*, P, *H*, *4,* and *8* (see Figure 1). The fundamental difficulty with all of them is the same as that recognized by Morse when he ruled out sequences of more than five dots in his first code. They are sources of sometimes ineradicable confusion. For example, *6,* unless it occurs in a context of numbers, is commonly mistaken for *P*. *P,* when alone or in cipher, may often be called *H; H* may be called *S; 4* may be called *V*; and *8* may be called *B.*

Down through the years, telegraphers became increasingly aware of this difficulty, but they seldom complained. There was little notion of either the prevalence of such confusions or of the direction that they most commonly took (*6* may be called *P,* but *P* is less likely to be called *6,* etc.). Some operators, having a good ear or a very quick wit, seemed to have no trouble. Others, less gifted, were often plagued by their failures to discriminate. With the advent of the semi-automatic key or "bug," early in this century, even the experts got into trouble once in awhile. The bug could be adjusted to provide very high rates of dotting. It was not only hard for the receiver to copy these dot signals, it was hard for the sender to transmit them accurately. Most *receivers* met the problem by relying upon context. The word *Please* does not begin with an *H*; *both* is not spelled b-o-t-s; and *March 1P* is not a date on any calendar. *Senders* met their problem in different ways. Sometimes they just "turned on *P* and let it run" for 10 dots or more. At other times, they shifted from bug- to hand-sending at critical points, and so on. All this took place day after day, year after year, in every busy railroad or commercial telegraph office of our country. Telegraphy became, on occasion, a high-tension performance, comparable to that provided by Pavlov when he pushed his dogs to the limit of their discriminative powers; but there was scarcely a murmur of protest from those most deeply involved.

Things might have been different if the telegraphers, or their employers, had read the psychological literature of the day. For example, they might have found in the British journal, *Mind,* for 1886, an interesting report from the Psychophysical Laboratory of Johns Hopkins University.[3] The writers of the report were two young men who were to become well-known in American psychology. Their names were G. Stanley Hall and Joseph Jastrow. They had conducted an experiment in which their subjects were asked to count the number of clicks made by a quill toothpick as it passed over cogs on the perimeter of a revolving metal plate. The number of clicks ranged from 2, at the bottom of the scale, up to as many as 65, at the top. The subjects made anywhere from three to ten judgments for each click number and at several rates of clicking.

Hall and Jastrow permitted each subject in this experiment to listen to each click sequence as many times as he wished, until he felt that his estimate of click number could not be improved. He was free to use every device of counting or grouping that he could think of in reaching an accurate estimate. But, in spite of all this, *underestimation of click number was clearly present in every instance.* Practice reduced the error considerably but did not eliminate it. Hall and Jastrow point out that the addition of a single click, even to as small a group as three, demands that the interval between clicks be increased appreciably if the larger number is to be reported correctly. Clearly, the poor telegrapher, often compelled to cope with just as fast a rate of clicking, but without benefit of more than an occasional immediate repetition of click number, would have felt underprivileged after reading such an account; and this was before the bug had been invented!

The Hall-Jastrow study was inspired by some observations at Hopkins on the reading and counting of visual trains of letters. These observations were made by James McKeen Cattell, fresh from Leipzig, where Wundt had become interested in the rhythms imposed by subjects as they listened to various rates of uniform beats. One of Wundt's pupils, Georg Dietze, had published on this topic a year in advance of the Hall-Jastrow paper (which was itself entitled *Studies of Rhythm*). In 1894, after Hall had moved to Clark, Thaddeus Bolton, one of his pupils, came out with a study much like Dietze's. This was followed, more or less directly, by the rhythm studies of Meumann, Koffka, Stetson, and, especially, Woodrow. Curiosity about mere error in judging auditory number was easily stifled by this interest in more dramatic phenomena. More than sixty years were to pass before any psychologist turned into the path suggested by the Hopkins study.

Revival of interest in this problem came at the outset of World War II. The setting was a very practical one. Good radio operators were needed for war work at a rate faster than they could be turned out by the service schools. There was particular interest in reducing the time required for teaching men and women to receive International Morse code.

This code, earlier known in this country as *Continental,* because of its origin, was a variation of American Morse that had been adopted for our military use prior to World War I. It differed from Morse's code in two major respects, as may be noted in Figure 1. It did away with the larger intra-signal spaces, as in *C, O, R, Y,* and *Z,* and it also offered an orderly arrangement of signals for the digits from *1* to *0.* As for the old dot problem of American Morse, you will note that the worst offender, the signal for *6,* is gone. Yet, a glance at the signals for *5, 4,* and *6* of the new code may suggest that the problem had not yet been completely solved.

There was, however, no evidence from the training centers to support such an expectation; nor was there any from the body of code-learning data that had been collected since World War I. As late as 1943, in Taylor's[18] review of the literature in the field, there was no more than the barest of recognitions that some signals were harder to deal with than others.

The first classroom research on the difficulty of the signals in International Morse code came as the outgrowth of a new method—the "code-voice" method—of teaching the code.[6] This method was developed at Columbia University during the period from 1941 to 1943. It was a form of the paired-associates procedure and consisted of three basic steps: (1) sounding a code signal in the ear of a student; (2) giving him three or four seconds in which to write down a letter or digit; and (3) telling him the correct name of the signal. The student printed his letters and digits (and the corrections when required) on a special practice sheet. A sample form of this sheet is shown in Figure 2, filled in from an actual record.

An entry within the upper square of any block of ten like those shown in the figure represents the student's response to the signal *before* it was identified. No entry means no response. An entry in the lower square of any block is made only when the response to the signal has been incorrect or did not occur. Thus, in response to the first signal, the student in this case wrote *0* when he should have written *S*. In response to the second signal, he wrote *A,* correctly; and he failed to respond to the third signal at all before his instructor said "Two"; and so on, throughout the 100-signal run, in which this student made 83 errors of omission or substitution.

This method can provide something more than a running account of a student's progress in terms of per cent correct. It can also tell him, after a bit, exactly where his trouble lies in learning—which signals are hard and which are easy, and which ones are mistaken for which others. Moreover, it gives his instructor the same information, making it possible for him to measure the relative difficulty of signals for the entire class. It may not surprise you to hear that two studies of signal difficulty were carried out before the first account of the code-voice method itself had been published.

In one of these studies, Spragg[15] examined the responses of 19 students in a code class at Queens College. The signals were machine-sent and for the alphabet characters only. In the other study, at Columbia University, Keller and Taubman[7] used 50 subjects, hand-sending, and all 36 signals. Both studies took their subjects well above the point of mere mastery of the code signals.

In Table 1 are shown the rank orders of difficulty provided by these two studies, together with one from a slightly later investigation by Plotkin.[10] Plotkin's study used 20 subjects, hand-sending, and all 36

Figure 2. Sample Code-Voice Practice Sheet

Name _____ Date _____ Time _____

| O A S V | H 3 N | H E H 4 | A N H N V | N S B |
| S 2 D 4 | L 7 J G P | F Q | T U M | R B W X |

| J ø L | X | N H N Z A | Z B L D | 2 O X |
| K 8 Z 3 | 5 C I 9 | A Z C L M | R Y D 7 W | I U P |

| A 7 E H | ø H | 2 T N 9 V | C T | ø H 9 H 9 |
| Q E 8 T B | C G 4 3 6 | T H A | J F K 5 O | Q R ø |

| E U T | N W E W | N O X C L | 2 H R T | V ø T |
| T U 7 K X | 8 M C D | Q R 4 | 3 G Y J | 5 W B 6 |

85

44

signals. The correlations between these rankings, based on alphabet errors of substitution only, are high: +.91 between the Spragg and Keller-Taubman ranks, and +.82 between the Plotkin and Keller-Taubman ranks.

These rank orders possess one puzzling feature. In view of my remarks about the defects of American Morse and the errors in judging auditory number, the rankings reflect very little trouble with signals containing strings of dots. Why, especially, is the signal for *H* (four dots) so easy to learn? It is 17th in Spragg's list, 16th in the Keller-Taubman list, and 12th in Plotkin's.[21]

With respect to this question, several points may be made. First, only the alphabet confusions are considered in these rank orders, since Spragg did not use the digit signals. Hence, the highest number of dots in any signal was *four,* and we would look for less difficulty with this number in the absence of a higher one (five) for which it might be mistaken. When we take into account *all* the signals, as in the Keller-Taubman and Plotkin studies, we find that confusions of *5* with *H, H* with *S, 6* with *B,* and *4* with *V* actually do account for about one-fifteenth of the substitution errors. Also, in terms of most frequently confused *pairs* of signals, *6-B, 5-H,* and *H-S* are among the four top pairs in each study.

Secondly, we might suspect that accurate judgments of auditory number would be related to reaction time, as Saltzman and Garner found for simultaneously shown visual dots. Greater difficulty would then be expected for dot signals later on in training. Quicker reactions would be required as the signals came in ever quicker succession. Finally, it might be that dotting errors would persist for a longer time than other errors.

Support for such thinking as this soon came from an extensive investigation by Seashore and Kurtz,[13] working on a wartime Navy project. These men carried the error analysis into later stages of training in code reception. Classes in Navy code schools were tested periodically with the project's standard proficiency tests.[8] The tests were given at different speed levels beyond basic code training, and all records of 80 per cent accuracy or better were examined for signal confusions. The findings, after 2, 4, 8, and 12 weeks of training showed a fairly constant rank order of difficulty. There was a *low* correlation (+.26) of their rank order with that obtained by Keller and Taubman, and, among the very most difficult signals at each stage of progress, were the following: *6, 5, 4, B, H,* and *V*—all of them 'dot signals.'

In addition to this, the *direction* of error was primarily toward *under-estimation.* Seashore and Kurtz remark that "the most interesting trend seen in the data . . . can be called the *signal-shrinkage phenomenon,* that is, a tendency for the student to hear code signals as being shorter than they are." They go on to suggest that special attention should be given to those

*Table 1. Rank Orders Of Difficulty in Mastering the Alphabet
Signals of International Morse Code
(Ranks Based on Substitution Errors Only)*

Rank	Keller-Taubman	Spragg	Plotkin
1 (most difficult)	W	Y	P
2	P	P	L
3	Y	X	W
4	Q	W	J
5	G	Q	Y
6	L	U	G
7	U	J	F
8	X	F	X
9	C	C	Q
10	D	L	Z
11	J	G	U
12	F	Z	H
13	K	K	D
14	R	R	C
15	Z	D	K
16	H	B	R
17	B	H	B
18	N	A	V
19	S	V	N
20	M	I	O
21	A	N	S
22	O	M	I
23	I	S	M
24	T	T	T
25	V	O	A
26	E	E	E

signals that are so hard to copy without error—*6, 5, 4,* and so forth. Presumably this might be done in two different ways. We might arrange our practice material so that the "hard" signals came much oftener than the "easy" ones, thus giving our student more chance to practice on them. Or we might give special drills on the trouble makers, to sharpen the distinctions between them in the routine transmissions. Both possibilities have since been explored.

E. A. Jerome[4] examined test papers in a Signal Corps school for high-speed operators. He found that most of the failures to pass the daily tests were due to the same sort of confusions as noted by Seashore and Kurtz. "Remedial" drills were therefore constructed and given to certain students in an attempt to eliminate these errors. The drill material included such five-letter cipher groups as *HHSSH, BDBBD,* etc., and was used during one of the four daily hours of receiving practice. Result: the "remedial" device was not remedial, no advantage whatever accrued from the drill. Indeed, if the drill was carried on for more than a couple of weeks, it was harmful in its effect.

Within the past year, Sidman[14] compared the progress of two groups of beginners in receiving code. One group used as its practice material an equal frequency of all the signals, both letters and digits. The other group used material that was weighted for signal frequency in accordance with the supposed relative difficulty of the signals. The data from this study have not yet been closely scrutinized, but it is clearly to be seen that no difference in group progress occurred as a result of the different practice material.

This schoolroom type of research has had some degree of tie up with the laboratory. As early as 1943, Jerome had carried out an experiment at Columbia University in which six subjects were asked to judge the number of auditory dots (1 to 16 short tones) at seven different rates (from 3.6 to as high as 20.1 per second). He found that the per cent of correct judgments fell off markedly as the *number* of dots increased or as the *rate* of dotting went up.

Jerome's work, unfortunately, was never published, but his lead was soon followed by Taubman,[16] who had been helping to develop the code-voice method of training. Taubman had been impressed by the way in which immediate knowledge of response correctness had seemed to aid code learning, so he undertook to make a special study of its effect upon the dotting error. He asked his subjects to judge from 1 to 6 short tones (like those in Jerome's study) at rates of approximately 7, 8, and 9 dots per second. Four of his subjects were told, after each judgment, the correct number of dots, while three others worked without such knowledge. Both groups improved during their period of training, but the "reinforced" group was distinctly superior, in terms of mean *judged number* and mean *per cent correct.* All subjects underestimated dot number from beginning to end of the experiment, but *overestimation* also appeared in the case of those subjects who worked with knowledge of their correctness. Taubman treated this as a compensatory effect arising from the subjects' awareness that they commonly erred in the opposite direction.

From this pilot study, Taubman went on, after the war, to a larger scale investigation of judged number, visual as well as auditory. [17] In alternate practice sessions, short tones and short flashes of light were presented to subjects at five different rates. The number ranged from 1 to 10. The auditory rates were from 6 to 9 per second, approximately, and the visual rates were from 2 to 5. Each subject judged each stimulus number at each rate 25 times.

Again the results showed that the accuracy of judging number decreases with (1) an increase in the stimulus number and (2) an increase in the rate. The more the dots, or the faster they come, the less the accuracy. The error is, once more, an error of *under-*, rather than *overestimation.* And now we know that these findings are not restricted to auditory dots alone, they hold for visual dots as well.

Taubman's data thus support his own earlier observations. They support Jerome's observations and they support those made by Hall and Jastrow 67 years ago. But this is not all. They have in turn been supported, and extended, by two further investigations, one of which was made, appropriately, at Johns Hopkins, where the experiments began.

W. R. Garner[2] employed short tones, of two intensities and two durations, and from 1 to 20 in number. He presented these tones at five different rates: 4, 6, 8, 10, and 12 per second. His data show again the effect of rate and number upon accuracy of judgment, with the same error of underestimation. (No influence of tonal intensity or duration appeared.) He did, however, note one factor not previously emphasized, that of wide individual differences. Some of his subjects could not count accurately more than four successive tones even at a repetition rate of four per second; ". . . the best quarter of the group could count as accurately at a rate of eight per second as the poorest quarter could at a rate of four per second."

The second follow-up of Taubman's study was in an experiment by Cheatham and White,[1] in the U. S. Navy Electronic Laboratory. These investigators went beyond Taubman's highest rate of 5 dots per second to rates of 10, 15, 22.5, and 30 per second of light flashes, and had subjects judge from 1 to 20 flashes at each rate. Once more number and rate are reflected in erroneous response, and there is still a striking underestimation of number, even for two flashes when the rate is high. But something new comes in. The relation between judged number and stimulus number shows rather well-defined steps. This is especially true when the flashes come at a rate of 30 per second. At this rate, 4 and 5 flashes will generally be reported as *two*; 8, 9, or 10 flashes will be reported as three; 14 and 15 will be called *four* and 18 and 19 will usually be called *five*. Other, intermediate, flash numbers will be divided between these judgment categories. Surprisingly enough, the judgments of number were made *easily* and *consistently.* Thus, when 9 flashes were presented at a 30-per-second rate, a subject might report that he saw three clear and distinct flashes. More accurately, there were three *pulsations*—expansions and contractions of light such as those described by Kenkel in 1913 and called "gamma movement." According to Cheatham and White, this reported number is "dependent on both the number of flashes presented and the total time in which they are presented."

Here, then, is a new development. It will undoubtedly receive further experimental attention and be related in due time to other visual phenomena. In addition, it may eventually bear upon the comparatively neglected practical problem of receiving Morse code when it is transmitted by blinker. Visual code reception may be more than a slowed-down version of auditory code reception.

These are the only research data that I have to report at this time on the problem of judging stimulus number. Before leaving the problem, however, I would like to consider it briefly in a different context.

Accurate reports of stimulus number and accurate reactions to Morse-code signals are basically matters of stimulus discrimination. On this I think we would all agree. In responding adequately to the code signals, a student must make at least 36 different responses, one for each of the 36 different stimuli. However, as in the case of many discriminations within a single sense modality, these stimuli, at the start of training, are easily confused with one another. When we increase the probability of a specific response to one stimulus, we also increase the probability of the same response to another stimulus. This is done on the basis of whatever properties the two stimuli share between them. For example: when we strengthen the response "C" to the signal for C, we also strengthen, to a lesser degree, the response "C" to the signal for Y. And so on. This is what, in present-day behavioral terms, we call "generalization." Learning to tell the signals apart requires the *breakdown* of many such generalizations.

The breakdown of generalization is achieved for most of the Morse-code signals in perhaps 8 or 10 hours of practice. One little cluster of signals may, however, hold out much longer than the rest. The signals for 6, 5 and 4 persist in arousing the responses for B, H, and V respectively. In like manner, the signals for B, H, and V are sometimes mistaken for those belonging to D, S, and U. The *gradient* of generalization, we might say, extends primarily in one direction and for 'one dot' only. At least this is the case when the total number of dots is no more than four or five, and when the rate of dotting is not excessive.

This leads me to mention one further experimental study, by Kaufman, Lord, Reese, and Volkmann,[5] at Mount Holyoke College. In this study, subjects were presented briefly with visual patterns of dots, from 1 to 210 in number, and asked to report the number as quickly and as accurately as they could. This is the modern form of the Hamilton or Jevons type of experiment.

One of the important findings of this study was a sharp discontinuity in the functions relating stimulus number to the time required for report, and to the confidence with which the report was made. In both cases, the break in the curves appeared at the same place—close to the point for *six stimulus dots.* This discontinuity led Kaufman and her associates to a distinction between three kinds of discriminative judgment: *estimating, subitizing,* and *counting. Estimating* is treated as a report of numerousness when the stimulus number is greater than six. *Subitizing* (from the Latin, *subitare, to arrive suddenly*) is applied to the discrimination of six, or less than six, stimuli. *Counting* is said to occur "when the stimulus-dots are presented in one place at a sufficiently low rate; when they are simultaneously presented in different places and are kept there; when they appear successively, in different places, and at a low rate." They point out that, in counting, a person makes one response for each one of a group of N objects, whereas in subitizing or estimating, a single response is given to an entire group of N objects.

In relation to the experiments that I have reviewed here, all three of these processes have probably been involved at one place or another. In some cases, where rates have been very slow, *counting* has undoubtedly occurred. In others, particularly when high dot numbers have been used, there must have been *estimating.* With high speed and low dot number, *subitizing* has probably been the rule. This is perhaps the usual case with Morse code, where the signal number does not exceed five dots and the speed is often too fast for counting.

Subitizing does not, unfortunately, guarantee accuracy. We have seen that even as few as two or three dots may be underestimated if the rate is high; and five may be called four, even with low rates. Moreover, there are wide individual differences. This point was made by Garner, and may be confirmed in any code school. There are some trainees who will err in judging number when the rate is that of manual tapping, others will subitize successfully at rates much higher. Small as this generalization gradient may be, it cannot be eliminated by any known method of training. We seem to be dealing with a threshold problem, sometimes a very upsetting one. And, as in the Pavlovian case, we may find 'neurotic' symptoms in our students as they approach the peak of their performance. "Code neurosis," a term that grew up in the training camps of the last war, is not an empty phrase.

These individual differences suggest, at the practical level of Morse-code learning, that we might well construct a test of code aptitude that would take them into account. This is a real possibility. It was partially recognized by Thurstone,[19] in 1943, but was laid aside before it had been fully explored. It has also been suggested in two or three of the papers I have cited in this talk. Within the past year, in fact, a preliminary form of such a device has been tried out on a small scale, with results that seem to warrant further work in this direction.

Still another possibility has been suggested by one or two workers in this field—most forcibly, and most recently, by Taubman.[17] It is unlikely that this possibility will ever be realized, but it would certainly not take more than one large-scale piece of institutional research to decide upon its practicability. The proposal, simply stated, is this: *Why not change the International Morse code?* Why not, in the interest of easy and effective communication, replace three signals of the code and thereby eliminate most of the discriminative problems associated with it? The three signals, of course, would be those for the letters *B, H,* and *V,* the letters that stand squarely in the troublemaking spot between *6, 5,* and *4,* on the one hand, and *D, S,* and *U* on the other. Take away these three offenders and you would at the same time take away most of the pain involved in acquiring and employing the International Morse code!

There are three especially good candidates for these positions. They are:

```
. _ . _
. . _ _
_ _ _ .
```

Each is a four component signal that could easily be relieved from any duty in communication that it now performs. Each would assuredly be confused to some extent with one or more other signals during the code-learning process, but the discriminative problems that they raised would almost certainly not be lasting ones. And, anyhow, the wisdom of using them, and the manner of introducing them to radio operators throughout the world, could easily be tested in advance, at no great cost, in a suitably designed experiment. Samual Morse altered his code twice within ten years. Another, fairly extensive change has been made in it during the past century. There is no need to close our minds forever to the possibility of still another.

Notes

1. Cheatham, P. G. & White, C. T. Temporal numerosity: I. Perceived number as a function of flash number and rate. *Journal of Experimental Psychology*, 1952, *44*, 447-451.

2. Garner, W. R. The accuracy of counting repeated short tones. *Journal of Experimental Psychology*, 1951, *41*, 310-316.

3. Hall, G. S. & Jastrow, J. Studies of rhythm: I. *Mind*, 1886, *11*, 55-62.

4. Jerome, E. A. & Keller, F. S. A test of two "remedial" devices in high-speed code reception. O.S.R.D. Report 5365, 1945.

5. Kaufman, E. L., Lord, M. W. Reese, T. W. & Volkman, J. The discrimination of visual number. *American Journal of Psychology*, 1949, *62*, 498-525.

6. Keller, F. S. Studies in International Morse code: I. A new method of teaching code reception. *Journal of Applied Psychology*, 1943, *27*, 407-415.

7. Keller, F. S. & Taubman, R. E. Studies in International Morse code: II. Errors made in code reception. *Journal of Applied Psychology*, 1943, *27*, 504-509.

8. Kurtz, A. K., Seashore, H. Stuntz, S. E. & Willits, J. M. The standardization of code speeds. O.S.R.D. Report 3490, 1944.

9. Morse, E. L. *Samuel F. B. Morse—His Letters and Journals.* Vol. II. New York: Houghton Mifflin, 1914.

10. Plotkin, L. Stimulus generalization in Morse code learning. *Archives of Psychology*, 287, 1943.

11. Prime, S. I. The Life of Samuel F. B. Morse, L.L.D. Inventor of the electro-magnetic recording telegraph. New York: Appleton, 1875.

12. Saltzman, I. J. & Garner, W. R. Reaction time as a measure of span of attention. *Journal of Psychology*, 1948, *25*, 227-241.

13. Seashore, H. & Kurtz, A. K. Analysis of errors in copying code. O.S.R.D. Report 4010, 1944.

14. Sidman, M. Personal communication.

15. Spragg, S. D. S. The relative difficulty of Morse code alphabet characters learned by the whole method. *Journal of Experimental Psychology*, 1943, *33*, 108-114.

16. Taubman, R. E. The effect of practice with and without reinforcement on the judgment of auditory number. *Journal of Experimental Psychology*, 1944, *34*, 143-151.

17. Taubman, R. E. Studies in judged number: I. The judgment of auditory number. II. The judgment of visual number. *Journal of General Psychology*, 1950, *43*, 167-219.

18. Taylor, D. W. Learning telegraphic code. *Psychological Bulletin*, 1943, *40*, 461-487.

19. Thurstone, L. L. Report on a code aptitude test. 1943. Privately Printed.

20. Woodworth, R. S. *Experimental Psychology*. New York: Holt, 1938.

21. The greater difficulty of H in Plotkin's study (as well as the relatively low correlation between the Keller-Taubman and the Plotkin ranks) may be due to the fact that Plotkin took as his measure of difficulty, not the number of errors made on each signal prior to mastery of the entire code, but the number of times each signal was presented before three successive correct responses were made to it.

5

The Phantom Plateau

Among the most often cited and best regarded studies in the psychology of skill are those of Bryan and Harter on American Morse-code learning. Since the beginning of this century, their work has been uncritically accepted by the textbook writers of our science. Which is strange when one considers that neither their procedures nor materials were ever described in any detail, and that their findings do not jibe with those from later studies. Only the plausibility of their theory of language-habit hierarchy seems to have sustained them through the years.

Early in our work on Morse code at Columbia it became apparent that the Bryan and Harter studies needed reexamination in the light of later data, but there were more urgent problems to consider at that time. It was not until the summer of 1955 that I had the opportunity to "repeat" their famous studies (or one of them at least), with my daughter, Anne, as an experimental subject, in a nostalgic farewell to the glamorous occupation of my youth. The following account was my Presidential Address to the Eastern Psychological Association in April 1957.

This paper is reprinted from the *Journal of the Experimental Analysis of Behavior,* 1958, *1,* 1-13. It is reprinted with permission of the *Journal of the Experimental Analysis of Behavior.*

Not so long ago I overheard a laboratory assistant in general psychology telling one of the boys in his section about a file of old examinations that we keep in the college library for students to consult. He ended brightly with the comment that it wouldn't do much good to study these exams. "You see," he said, "we use the same questions from year to year, but we change the answers."

This disturbed me at the time. It seemed like a dangerous quip to make. What if word got around that we actually did change our answers? Might we not be investigated for Unacademic Activities? A little reflection, however, suggested that changing answers was, in truth, a sign of good health in any course of study. It suggested, too, that such changes are really quite uncommon—especially in the beginning course. And, finally, it suggested a few answers that ought to be changed. One of these makes up the burden of the present discussion.

The answer to which I refer is commonly given in textbook chapters on learning, or habit-formation. Under such headings, it may fall within a treatment of skill, practice, or, occasionally, learning-curve plateaus.

In conformity with a well-known teaching procedure, the question itself comes after the answer, usually by several weeks. In an old-fashioned essay-type examination, it might read like this:

> What is the normal course of progress in the mastery of a skill? How might a curve for ball-tossing or pursuit-meter learning differ from that for Morse code receiving? Explain this difference. (10 points)

An A student's answer to this question might go as follows:

> The progress curve for most skills is negatively accelerated. The amount of improvement from one trial to the next decreases as the number of trials increases. This is true of ball tossing and of keeping contact with the target of a pursuit meter. However, progress in Morse code receiving typically shows a long period of no advance—a *plateau*—midway in training. This plateau occurs only in the case of receiving plain-language material. It is said to be due to the fact that code proficiency depends on learning to respond to phrases and sentences as units, rather than to letters or words. The plateau represents the period in which word habits have not yet become sufficiently automatic for progress with phrases and sentences to take place.

This is the answer that I would like to change. It is wrong in two respects. First, the receiving curve for plain-language Morse code does *not* typically show a plateau. Secondly, our student has offered a faulty analysis of the receiving process. Since both errors are widespread, and since the second reaches well beyond a purely Morse code problem, it will be my aim, in what follows, to suggest some corrections.

All of you have seen the receiving curve to which our student refers. It has been a standard fixture of our textbooks for more than half a century. It is sometimes found in company with a sending curve, and sometimes with two other receiving curves. My first two figures will refresh your memory.

Figure 1. From General Consensus of Operator's Opinions

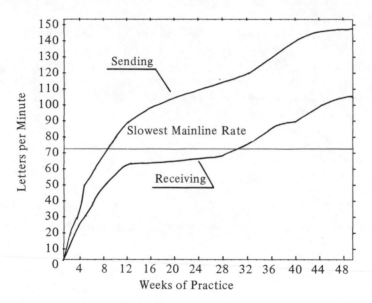

In Figure 1, this receiving curve appears as the lower one of the two. The upper one is for progress in sending. In each case, code speed, in letters per minute, is plotted against weeks of practice. The line drawn parallel with the base indicates the lowest acceptable speed for practical communication—72 letters per minute. Just below this line is the famous plateau, extending throughout most of a 16-week period.

Figure 2 contains a similar plot. The plain-English receiving curve is here the upper one. The next curve below is for receiving disconnected words, and the bottom curve is for receiving disconnected letters. The plateau appears only in the plain-language curve.

58

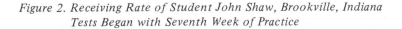

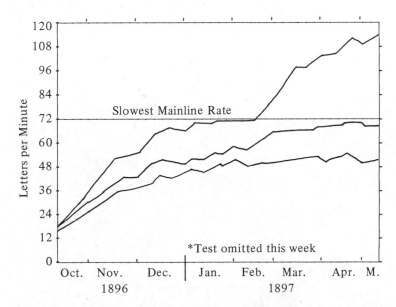

The two studies from which these curves were taken are classics in the psychology of skill.[1,2] Both were published in the *Psychological Review*, one in 1897 and the other in 1899; and both resulted from the joint endeavor of two men: *William Lowe Bryan* and *Noble Harter*. Bryan, the senior author, was then professor of psychology at Indiana University; Harter, an ex-telegrapher, was a graduate student working under Bryan's direction.

The 1897 Bryan and Harter paper contained the first known records of advancement in sending and receiving Morse code. These records were obtained in several ways. First, Harter cross-examined 37 railway and commercial telegraphers, asking them about their experience in mastering the code. From their answers he was led to construct the pair of curves that are shown in Figure 1. Four more pairs of "typical" curves were drawn from data supplied by schools of telegraphy with which he made contact. There is no need to present them here, since they are practically identical with the pair that you can see. This is also true of two pairs that were collected by friends of Harter's—railway telegraphers, each of whom tested weekly the progress of a student in his office.

Then Harter got some first-hand information. He tested for himself the weekly progress of two young students in the Brookville, Indiana, Western

Union office. The results are pictured in Figures 3 and 4. Except for their greater irregularity, they are like all the others, especially in showing the same receiving-curve plateau at a point just below the main-line level of acceptability.

Figure 3. Student Edyth L. Balsley, Tested Weekly by Noble Harter at W. U. Telegraph Office, Brookville, Indiana

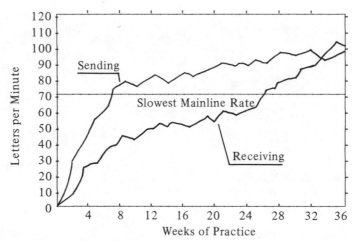

In their first paper, Bryan and Harter point out the existence of this plateau in all of their receiving curves for connected discourse. They note that many students become discouraged at this level of their code-receiving proficiency. They suggest that foreign-language learning goes through a similar phase of no improvement. But they do not tell us why the plateau occurs.

In 1899, they went further. They began with a report of some new findings. Harter had followed the progress of John Shaw, a student in the Brookville office, from the 6th through the 35th week of code practice. Shaw had been tested every Saturday, in sending and receiving. The receiving tests made use of three kinds of material: disconnected letters, disconnected words, and connected words—i.e., plain English.

Three receiving curves were generated from these tests. Observe once more the curves of Figure 2. The uppermost, plain-language curve resembles all the earlier curves that had been plotted. The same plateau is there, with a main-line breakthrough at about the same place as before, in the 24th week of practice. The word and letter curves, however, appear to have reached their limit of advance. This limit, even for the curve of disconnected words, is well below the main-line requirement of 72 letters per minute.

60

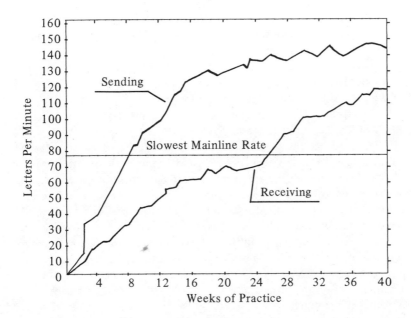

Figure 4. *Student Will J. Reynolds, Tested Weekly by Noble Harter at W. U. Telegraph Office, Brookville, Indiana*

The second aim of the 1899 paper was to explain the plateau. Bryan and Harter had by this time questioned more telegraphers; they had considered the way in which blind children read Braille; they had heard of a "period of depression" in learning college chemistry; and, especially, they had John Shaw's word and letter curves to think about.

The result of all this is now an old story, but still appealing. It runs as follows. In learning Morse code, one acquires a *hierarchy of habits.* Letters must first be mastered; then syllables and words; and finally, phrases and sentences. Mastery of the higher-order habits depends on mastery of the lower-order ones. To receive sentences, that is, one must first have acquired the component word-habits; to receive words, one must have acquired the letter-habits.

As for the plateau, let us go straight to Bryan and Harter:[2]

> A plateau in the curve means that the lower-order habits are approaching their maximum development, but are not yet sufficiently automatic to leave the attention free to attack the higher-order habits.

As the receiving curve ascends from the base line, "no plateau appears between the learning of letters and of words, because very soon these are learned simultaneously." It takes a large vocabulary of words, however, before one can form the phrase and sentence habits needed for high-speed receiving; hence the plateau. When the vocabulary has become automatic, the curve ascends for the second time, to a level that marks the peak of achievement for most telegraphers.

Bryan and Harter have little to say about those who go still higher, beyond noting that "complete freedom in the telegraphic language" is reached only after years of apprenticeship, and comes as suddenly as did the ascent from the first plateau. Presumably, this depends upon one's mastery of language units that are highest in the habit hierarchy.

There were some puzzling features of these two papers. More puzzling today, perhaps, than they were in 1890. For example, there is the remarkable resemblance of all the receiving curves in the first Bryan and Harter report. We know, from the more recent studies, that progress in receiving the International form of Morse code is affected by many factors. It depends on the number of hours of practice per day; on the content of the practice materials employed; on the criteria of perfection used in passing a student from one speed to another; on the size of the steps in practice speed; and so on, and on. We know, too, that progress curves from different schools today are often quite unlike. Was there more uniformity of procedure in the code schools of the '90's than in those of our time? Is American Morse less affected by these variables than International Morse? Or, was Thorndike[6] (page 285) right when he suggested that the similarity of the Bryan and Harter curves was due to the inadequacy of the questionnaire used in collecting the data?

Then, in the second paper, there is the matter of John Shaw's curves for receiving disconnected words and letters. Why did these curves never reach the main-line level? Even in those days there must have been telegraphers who copied stock-market reports and ciphered messages at speeds higher than 72 letters per minute. In Signal Corps schools today, even low-speed operators receive mixed letters and digits at rates well above this; and high-speed operators, using typewriters, reach nearly twice that rate. Had this student really reached his limit? Or did he fail to go further because he had so little chance to copy disconnected words and letters in his daily practice sessions?

We shall never know the answers to such questions. But for a brief mention of the manner in which Harter conducted the test in the Brookville office, they tell us nothing about training methods, practice material, steps in speed, criteria of passing, or any other influence that might be at play. For more light upon such matters, we must await the studies of later men.

The investigation of code learning requires an intimate acquaintance with a rather unusual training situation. It depends on more than a casual interest in practical goals. Also, it requires special experimental subjects—young men or women on whom one can rely for long-term class attendance and high motivation. It is for these reasons that war time has been the best time for research in this field. There is then a shortage of men with code skill. Investigators are then willing to work long and hard in the interest of the purely useful; and the government is usually ready to help them with funds and facilities. Experimental subjects, often in uniform, are plentiful and tractable.

The first major attack on the Bryan and Harter position came in World War I. It was made by Rees Edgar Tulloss,[7] at Harvard University, as part of a doctoral dissertation entitled "The Learning Curve—with Special Reference to the Progress of Students in Telegraphy and Typewriting." In the code-learning field, this was a very important study; yet, for some reason, it was never published. In fact, its existence was barely noted until early in World War II. At that time, Donald W. Taylor, [5] another Harvard code researcher, dug it out of Widener Library for a *Bulletin* review.

In the section of his dissertation that deals with telegraphy, Tulloss offers us, first, an improved method of testing speed in code receiving—a method in which each test was based on two or three short runs of signals, sent at each of several different speeds, and including as many as four distinct types of test material. There were runs of English text, in which all the letters of the alphabet were represented; there were runs of disconnected letters, covering the alphabet, but with a frequency of appearance like that in plain English. Finally, there was a special test, called "alphabetical code," in which the 26 letters were represented randomly in each of two or three alphabet runs.

Using one or more of these tests, Tulloss measured the weekly progress of 23 students in International Morse code, including 19 from a Navy school that had been set up at Harvard. The latter were tested, during most of their training, with all four kinds of test material, along with a plain-language test that was given by the school itself.

Three members of this class had no prior experience with any form of Morse code when they started training. The record for one of these men was clearly atypical, for known reasons. The other two records were remarkably alike, and typified the progress of the entire group throughout most of the training period.

One of the two provided the data for Figure 5. Letters per minute are here plotted against weeks of practice, with about 20 hours of practice to the week. Progress is most rapid at the start, followed by a slower, fairly straight-line advance, or a slight deceleration up to the end of training. All

Figure 5

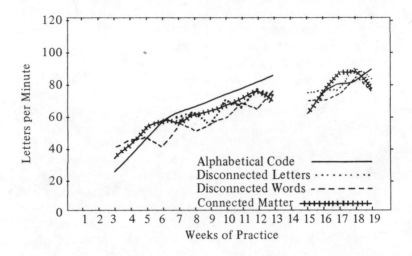

Figure 6

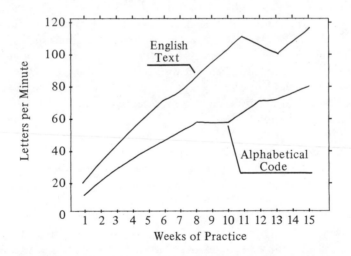

of the curves reach a level well above the Bryan and Harter main-line speed—even in the case of disconnected letters, as in Tulloss' alphabetical code. Finally, except for one or two obviously abnormal records, there is *no sign of a plateau* in any of the Tulloss curves—plain-language or otherwise.

These curves are, of course, for progress in International Morse, a code that differs from American Morse in two important ways. Its signals are composed of long and short tones, rather than patterns of clicks; and six of its letter signals are different from those of the older code in their dot-dash construction. Hence, one might fairly argue that Tulloss had no right to expect a confirmation of the Bryan and Harter findings.

To meet this objection, Tulloss measured the progress of four students of American Morse, in a special class at Simmons College. As test material, he used only the alphabetical code, although the Western Union instructor of the class added his own weekly tests with plain-language material.

These students received approximately 10 hours of practice every week, and all four of them went ahead at about the same pace. The record for the slowest student of the group, throughout her 15 weeks of study, is shown in the two curves of Figure 6. These curves, and those from the other three subjects, are like the ones obtained with the International code. Even the slowest student shows a fairly steady climb in speed with disconnected letters to a point beyond that reached by John Shaw; and we see again that plain-language receiving may pass the main-line test without the appearance of a plateau.

The Tulloss studies did much to advance our knowledge of Morse-code learning. They were not, however, without flaws, one of which Tulloss himself had found in Bryan and Harter. In trying to account for their plateau, he concluded that it was due to lack of practice with the more difficult signals of the code. Yet, in his own work, except in the case of one student whose only training came while taking tests, there was no control of the practice materials employed. His results, it might be argued, were equally a function of an unknown state of affairs.

The code researches of World War II were free from this defect. In service schools, especially, both practice and test materials were commonly specified from start to finish of a student's training. As a rule, however, they lacked variety, being restricted mainly to military cipher, with little or no plain-language code. It was not until 1953, 35 years after Tulloss' work, that the problem of practice materials was faced in an adequate manner.

The study to which I refer was conducted at Columbia University, under Air Force contract, by Donald A Cook.[3] Its aim was to measure progress in receiving International Morse code when students were not only tested, but trained, with five different kinds of material. These were as follows:

1. A *zero-order approximation* to ordinary English text—a random presentation of the 36 basic signals, in equal frequency, with punctuation

signals, and in word-like groupings. This is probably the most difficult material that an American code student has ever been asked to copy.

2. A *first-order* approximation to English, in which the signals for letters, digits, and punctuation again appeared randomly, but with a relative frequency like that of ordinary English.

3. A *second-order* approximation to English, comprising material in which the succession of letters was slightly more predictable than in the first-order case. Each letter had as its nearest neighbor a letter, a number, a space, or a mark of punctuation such as might be expected to occur in English text.

4. *Disconnected discourse,* another form of approximation, in which ordinary English *words* appeared, with a frequency close to that of their occurrence in our language, but in a scrambled sequence. This was probably similar to John Shaw's "disconnected words."

5. *English text,* which came from a variety of sources, mostly nonfiction. Cook's aim was to use material that was neither esoteric nor familiar, and to avoid selections of specialized interest.

All these materials were presented in *cycles.* Each cycle contained samples of everything then in use, at each of several speeds, and sent in runs of about 300 signals each. From these runs, for all the cycles, it was possible to construct progress curves of the Bryan and Harter type for every kind of material with which each student worked. The curves in Figure 7 are those for a student whose record was most like that for the group as a whole. In this graph, *E-zero, E-1,* and *E-2* refer, respectively, to *zero-order, first-order,* and *second-order* approximations to English. *Text,* obviously, refers to connected discourse. (The amount of training with disconnected discourse, for this subject, was not enough to provide a progress curve for such material.)

It is quickly apparent from these curves that progress went on quite steadily for each kind of material throughout the practice hours in which it was employed. There are ups and downs, as in the Tulloss curves, but nowhere do we find the classical plateau. Moreover, the old main-line speed is again, in every case, exceeded. This would be true even if we were to handicap the International code severely in making our comparisons.

In this graph, and most of the others, something else appears—something noted earlier by Tulloss, and in sharp contrast with the Bryan and Harter findings. That is, progress with text was actually slower than that for any other material except the zero-order approximation to English. To this matter I shall return in a moment.

From the findings of these two investigations, you will probably be led to agree that the answer should be changed to our original question about

Figure 7

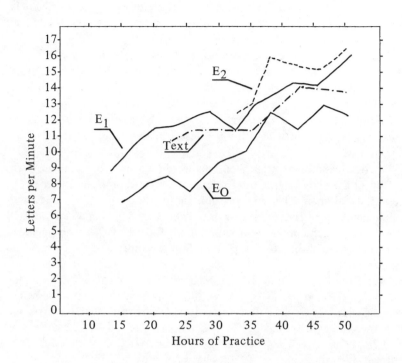

Figure 8

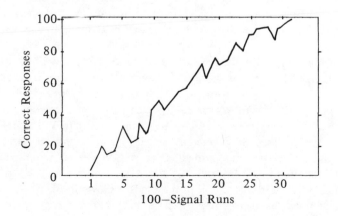

"the normal course of progress in the mastery of a skill," at least when this answer states that Morse code progress *typically* shows a plateau. There is, however, one more study to be noted here, as a sequel to the John Shaw story, and as one last look for the classical curve.

This study deals with the progress, in American Morse, of one experimental subject, who was given daily code practice during 10 weeks in the summer of 1955. This subject, Anne Simmons, was an 18-year-old high-school graduate who was working to earn money for college expenses. Her instructor, who shall be nameless, was an elderly ex-telegrapher, trained in American Morse, and with a lively interest in the proper conduct of the experiment.

Practice sessions for Anne Simmons were held on 7 days of the week, usually in the early afternoon. The practice material included four of the five kinds of material used by Cook in the study just described, with supplements from *Treasure Island* and *Tom Sawyer*. The material omitted was Cook's second-order approximation to English. Digits were included with the letters, as before, but punctuation was limited to the comma and the period.

Initial mastery of the 36 basic signals was brought about with the code-voice method.[4] This is a procedure in which the instructor names each signal a few seconds after sending it, and the student tries to respond with the correct letter or digit during the pause. All 36 of the signals were used from the start. They were sent in runs of 100 each, in random order, and with rest-pauses and error-tallies between runs.

For the first 12 days of training, this method was in effect, with one hour of practice daily. There were two 100-signal runs on the first day, and three on each day thereafter. The subject's progress throughout this phase of the study is portrayed in Figure 8. The number of correct responses per run is here plotted against the number of runs. The over-all picture is crudely linear, up to the point of near-perfection, but you will observe a cyclical effect that is clearly due, in the first half of training, to overnight losses of skill.

Then the speed runs were begun, for two hours a day and with all four types of material. The speed at the start was one of four words (20 letters) per minute. It was increased, in one-word-per-minute steps, as the subject met each passing criterion of 95-per cent correct copy in three runs for a given material. The runs were generally one minute long (never shorter) and, in all but a few cases, they were checked for errors by the "call-back" method immediately after being copied. Each run, in a sense, was treated as a test, and the subject was informed of each test score.

The subject's progress with the four materials is shown in Figure 9. For each week of practice, the point plotted on each curve is for the final speed reached and passed in that week. The lower curve, for E-zero (letters and digits in equal frequency), is a faintly undulating curve, barely deviating from a straight line. The upper three curves, for English text, disconnected words, and a first-order approximation to English, are negatively accelerated and almost indistinguishable from each other.

Figure 9

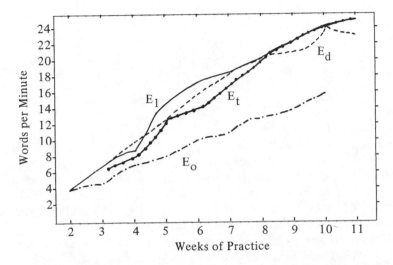

These curves, unlike Cook's, are based on American Morse, the code that Bryan and Harter studied. Unlike the Tulloss curves, they deal with the entire code and they result from a known and equal amount of practice on all the types of material with which the student was tested. Yet, in their appearance, they are little more than smoothed-out and speeded-up versions of the Cook and Tulloss curves. There is no plateau, at any place, for any kind of material. In addition, the curves for disconnected discourse and disconnected letters (plain-English frequency) reach heights that John Shaw never dreamt of.

To see this vividly, compare, in Figure 10, the records of Anne Simmons and John Shaw for plain English and disconnected words—materials that were probably nearest alike for the two students.

This little experiment was brought to an end, at a prearranged date, to provide the subject with a well-deserved vacation. It could have gone no further, anyhow, without drastic changes in procedure. Anne Simmons was close to her limit in speed of *handwriting,* and her instructor, using a standard telegraph key, was barely able to reach the topmost speeds employed with each material. By using a typewriter, and a higher speed

Figure 10

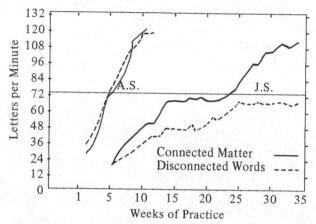

transmission of signals, the curves would surely have continued to climb. Perhaps they would have paused for a while in their ascent, on that *second* plateau of which Bryan and Harter made mention. Or perhaps they would have marched on, at a slowing pace, but steadily, into the realm of the expert. I would guess the latter, but I might be wrong. This is country into which no Morse code researcher has ever yet entered.

In 1918, having looked in vain for plateaus in all his progress curves, Rees Tulloss began to re-examine the code-receiving process. The result was a multi-stage analysis of this skill which has not yet been improved upon, and which I venture to outline here as an alternative to the Bryan and Harter view.

At the very start of training, according to Tulloss, the code beginner has usually memorized a list of visual dot-dash symbols, one for each letter and digit. Hence, his first response to an *auditory* signal is one of visualizing or covertly verbalizing its dot-dash elements. This reaction sets off, in turn, a subvocal articulation of the appropriate character; and this articulation is itself followed immediately by the copying response—the writing (or speaking) of the letter or digit. In every case of reaction to a signal, there is this little chain of events. In responding to a simple combination of a short and long tone, for example, a student might visualize a dot and a dash, utter subvocally the letter "a," and then write the letter down—all within a second or two of time.

As practice continues, however, several more things happen. First, the initial visualizing or verbalizing within each chain is replaced by a "duplicative" or "imitative" response. Instead of reacting to the tonal compound by saying "dot-dash" or seeing the dot and dash, the student says to himself something like "di-dah"—a muscular approximation to the tonal pattern. The complete sequence will then be as follows: (1) the auditory dot-dash; (2) the imitative "di-dah"; (3) the silent articulation of "a"; and (4) the copying response—the writing of "a."

With further practice, the duplicative response drops out of the chain. The signal pattern now leads directly to covert articulation of the letter, after which the copying response occurs. The reaction time of the copying response to each signal is thus appreciably shortened, first to the "easy" signals, and then to the "hard" ones, and the student's code speed is correspondingly increased.

The next main feature of the process, with still further practice, is one in which each response chain begins to *overlap* in time with its neighbors. The student is gradually enabled to begin a second, or even a third, linkage before the first one has come to its end. This permits, of course, another increase in his speed of receiving, and lets him "copy behind," at least by one or two letters.

You might imagine that the next advance would be another shortening of reaction time—that the middle link of each chain, the covert articulation of letters and digits, would then drop out, and that each signal would come to evoke, directly, the copying response. Tulloss would possibly have agreed that for students who deal mainly with meaningless transmissions of disconnected letters and numbers, something like this might really occur. But he would certainly have denied that the link drops out for those who go on to the next stage of the code-receiving process.

This stage is one of *word-articulation*. It is a kind of "spelling-out" stage, in which the articulation of letters is still a basic feature. Consider the case in which plain language is being sent. The signals come along as usual, one by one. Each signal continues to evoke the articulation of a letter—however fragmentary, however covert, this letter response may be. The letters, of course, spell out words, and if they come in close enough succession, they lead the student to say the words to himself. Thus, having subvocalized "t," "h," and "e," as the signals call these letters up, he finds himself, like any other speller, articulating "the." To each sequence of his own letter responses, he makes a single, unitary word response, even before he puts his pencil to the paper.

To appreciate this argument fully, and to get the feel of code receiving at high speed, you have only to listen to someone's dictation of the letters in a series of words, at a rate of two or three letters per second. The effect will be even better if you try to write the letters as the message is sent. For example, see if you can "copy" the following:

THISISASIMPLIFIEDVERSION

("This is a simplified version")

You can understand, after listening to this message, how unlikely it is that ten successive letters, as in the word "simplified," or seven, as in "version," could ever function as an auditory whole. There may be word *responses,* just as there are letter responses, but code signals are never word *stimuli,* except in the case of very short words or uncommonly high speeds.

You can also see how word articulations arise from the articulations of letters and must always depend upon them in the receiving process. These word responses are not compounds of letter responses, but are merely evoked by them, just as any response evokes another. Often the word response comes up before the letter chain has been completed. Some of you may have uttered "simple," subvocally, before the sixth letter of "simplified" had been spoken; or you may have articulated "version" before that word was half spelled. In the first case, a mistake was made, which may or may not have disrupted the receiving process. In the second case, no harm was done, since the letters that followed your precocious word response served simply to confirm it.

This "guessing" behavior occurs primarily in the case of plain-language or disconnected-word receiving. It is obviously related to one's spelling experience, and it probably accounts for the fact that progress with text and mixed words may actually be *slower* than with almost any other kind of material. As I have already noted, both Cook and Tulloss had students who gave them such results. In the case of Anne Simmons, there was no clear effect of this sort; but even at the end of her training she was still copying "close behind"—responding letter by letter to most of each transmission. Ultimately, in her case, as in others, we would expect words to be articulated in advance of being written. We would also expect that with increased knowledge of common pitfalls—the different ways in which letter sequences may get off the track—there would be fewer and fewer mistakes. Plain English would, in the end, be easiest to copy.

Tulloss goes two steps further in dealing with high-speed code reception. First, he argues for a second stage of overlapping, in which each of several word articulations may, at the same time, be in process of arousing its own copying response. He likens the process to that of ordinary writing, in which the word being written may be several words behind the one from which it stemmed. Secondly, he has something to say about the expert's ability to copy behind by 10 or 12 words or more:[7]

What we can and do have (here) is a present articulation of the word, without immediate writing response, and then later a *repeated* articulation of the word which does result in its writing. . . . The words are articulated as they are spelled out. They are remembered and repeated.

These analyses, however, carry less conviction than the earlier ones. In particular, Tulloss' appeal to "memory" in the final stage is not very helpful; and the need for repeating a word sequence before writing it is not very clear. One might just as plausibly argue that successive words, like successive letters, *directly* induce the writing of those familiar patterns to which they belong.

This is the Tulloss story, told briefly and, perhaps, with distortion. It is probably incorrect in detail, and it is certainly incomplete. It also assumes the existence of events that you may think of as undesirably subjective, as, for example, the subvocal articulation of letters, words, and "duplicative" responses. But nothing metaphysical is here involved; the private events differ from the public only in their magnitude, not in kind.

Tulloss did not explain the plateau because he had no plateau to explain; for him, the plateau was a phantom, or the outcome of bad training methods. But he did throw light on the Bryan and Harter doctrine. He helps us see how they could talk of receiving words and sentences, without asking us to believe that a series of 20 to 100 or more dots and dashes of code, requiring many seconds for transmission, may function as an auditory unit.

His analysis fits readily within the framework of modern reinforcement theory, and it suggests a much closer tie between code learning and other verbal activities than we have been wont to consider in the past. I am thinking of its relation not only to such skills as those of shorthand, typing, and reading Braille, but also to those involved in reporting, listening, and understanding. The theoretical gain that accrues from relating code to such transactions should be more than enough to compensate us for the loss of that mysterious power bequeathed by Bryan and Harter to the telegraphic art.

The further study of this problem need not involve Morse code at all. High-speed receiving is simply a form of taking dictation, and can be investigated with signals that are no more elaborate or unfamiliar than the spoken letters or words of our mother tongue. Indeed, the patterns of Morse code are but awkward, slow-moving, and hard-to-master counterparts of letters, digits, and marks of punctuation. For some rather special purposes, they may still be preferred. For others, we ought to employ their less-demanding mates. From the study of dictation, by letters and words, we might then move on, in orderly fashion, to verbal report and note-taking, testimony and rumor, and the "comprehension of ideas."

Notes

1. Bryan, W. L. & Harter, N. Studies in the physiology and psychology of the telegraphic language. *Psychological Review,* 1897, *4,* 27-53.

2. Bryan, W. L. & Harter, N. Studies on the telegraphic language. The acquisition of a hierarchy of habits. *Psychological Review,* 1899, *6,* 345-375.

3. Cook, D. A. Message type as a parameter of learning to receive International Morse code. Paper read at Eastern Psychological Association Meetings, New York, April, 1957.

4. Keller, F. S. Studies in International Morse code: I. A new method of teaching code reception. *Journal of Applied Psychology,* 1943, *27,* 407-415.

5. Taylor, D. W. Learning telegraphic code. *Psychological Bulletin,* 1943, *40,* 461-487.

6. Thorndike, E. L. *Educational psychology. Vol. 2. The psychology of learning.* New York: Teachers College, 1913.

7. Tulloss, R. E. The learning curve—With special reference to the progress of students in telegraphy and typewriting. Unpublished doctoral dissertation. Harvard University, 1918.

6

The Psychology Curriculum
at Columbia College

I am not sure when or where I first met William Nathan ("Nat") Schoenfeld, but I vividly recall one early contact, in a first-floor Schermerhorn classroom at Columbia, while he was still a graduate student. I went to hear a lecture by Professor Garrett,[1] on statistics, and Nat was his assistant. I sat down near him and we exchanged some pleasantries before the class began. I am sure I viewed him with respect since he, like many others at Columbia, seemed to know so much that I did not; but I am also sure that I had no inkling of the part he was to play in my academic life for many years to come.

Professor Garrett's reputation as a teacher I found to be entirely warranted, but other demands upon my time soon drew me away from his classes. My relationship with Nat Schoenfeld, however, was not thereby disrupted. We continued to see each other, with increasing frequency and profit. I introduced him to the *Behavior of Organisms* and found in him an avid, systematic thinker. It wasn't long before a friendship had developed.

Some people, to use the words of a former colleague, "destroy one's behavior." In their presence one is mute, or clumsy, or led to make silly statements. Conversations with them sag, recover, and sag again, in a depressing cycle. There is no fruitful interaction, intellectual or social. With Nat and me the opposite was true. In all our meetings and discussions, each of us seemed to call out the best that the other had to offer. Together we resonated to the *Behavior of Organisms;* together we worked on several code researches; and together we dreamed of a college program which would develop and extend the systematic outline that Skinner had provided for our science.

However, our duties in different branches of the Department discouraged more complete collaboration for some time.

Late in 1944, or early in 1945, while at Camp Crowder, I wrote a long letter to John Volkmann concerning a scheme for renovating Psychology 1-2 in Columbia College when we returned from the wars. This was the introductory course on which we had worked together after Gardner Murphy left for City College. I proposed, in brief, a laboratory course—one in which we would use white rats as subjects, with a systematic presentation of reinforcement theory at the first-course level. I asked for his opinion of the project.

In typically thorough fashion, John responded with a long and detailed letter, pointing realistically to the many problems that were involved. Later, in equally typical fashion, he offered his support for the entire undertaking. Within another year, when we were back in academic harness, we had secured the permission of our Chairman (Professor Garrett) and the hearty approval of the Dean (Harry J. Carman), together with $5,500 with which to start us on our way.

In a concerted effort, which involved not only Volkmann, but Thomas W. Reese, Donald H. Bullock, and Frederic C. Frick (then graduate students), as well as Fred Blendinger, our shop man, and one or two others, we were able to launch our course in the fall of 1946. At the very last moment, before our first class had actually met, Volkmann and Reese left for Mt. Holyoke College. Nat Schoenfeld stepped into the breach and saved us from disaster.

My debt to Nat in the years that followed cannot be exaggerated. He supplied the skills and knowledge that I lacked, as he had done in our Morse-code collaborations; and the course for which I usually get the credit owed more to him than it did to me. As for the present paper, it seems to me that Schoenfeld did more work than I did on it. I thank him for letting me use the paper here.

"The Psychology Curriculum at Columbia College," F. S. Keller and W. N. Schoenfeld, is reprinted from the *American Psychologist*, 1949, *4*, 165-172. It is reprinted with permission from the *American Psychologist* and W. N. Schoenfeld.

When, in September 1946, we introduced a new psychology curriculum at Columbia College, we were carrying out a long-incubated plan. Part of this plan, and something of its implementation, was described at the 1947 meeting of the EPA in Atlantic City. We are now in the third year of our venture and feel that it is time to give our fellow-teachers a more complete account. We sincerely hope that, as a result, they will favor us with their appraisals or comments.

It was during the war years that we began the discussions which led to our new program. By 1946-47, the necessary arrangements had been made and we were ready to set out. Initially, we focussed our attention on the introductory course, the keynoter of the curriculum, and the gauntlet which transient students and future colleagues alike must run. Later, as the first course seemed to prosper, we extended the idea to our advanced offerings, until nearly all the College courses were included within an integrated educational structure. The result has been highly satisfying. Whatever the ultimate outcome, we have found new pleasure in teaching and have been enabled, we believe, to give our pupils a sounder introduction to the science of psychology than we had provided before.

The Introductory Course. The teaching of the beginning course, as of any other, is grounded upon one's answers to the questions of *goal, content* and *form*—the Why, the What, and the How of teaching. When we took up the matter of goal, we found ourselves in good agreement with our colleagues. Like them, we wanted (1) to give our pupils some facts about the behavior of organisms; (2) to provide a coordinated picture rather than a patchwork of isolated items; (3) to instill a feeling for scientific method and research in psychology; (4) to help the student to apply, as well as possible, behavioral principles to his own and others' daily conduct; and (5) to arouse interest in the science as such, attracting the ablest students and preparing them for any advanced work they might later undertake. In these and other aims we were at one with our friends. It was only with respect to matters of content and form of the course that we found ourselves veering to a different direction. As to the What and the How, we felt that the usual introductory course was incapable of realizing its high purposes.

What to Teach? Ordinarily, the first course in psychology presents to the student a wide variety of topics, ranging from nervous-system function to personality and social interaction. An attempt is made to give the student a bird's eye view of the things studied by, or of interest to, psychologists. The choice of topics seems to be largely dependent upon custom, and the order of topics is more or less arbitrary.[2] Integration of the topics is seldom attempted. Indeed, it is impossible, in the present state of our knowledge, to relate within any known systematic framework the many problems offered to the student in the conventional presentation.

The choice of topics in such a course has often been defended by appeal to the virtues of eclecticism. But eclecticism is often misinterpreted to mean an absence of a coordinated viewpoint. We would contend that psychological theory today offers the opportunity to take just such a systematic stand. We are further convinced that many of our colleagues await only a crude approximation of a systematic text and an integrated curriculum before giving up their older ways of teaching. They do not like the encapsulation of topics, segregated one from the other by impenetrable theoretical barriers; they do not enjoy the citing of data unrelated by known and stated principles; and they are embarrassed by the fiction, transparent to the most naive student, that the conventional first course is a genuine prerequisite for advanced ones. They have not forgotten that systematization of data is the purpose of science; they deplore the fragmentation of knowledge; and their good scientific sense does not hold with what often comes trippingly off their tongues.

Our own approach is not eclectic in the above sense. One who insists upon classifying theoretical psychologists into "schools" would unhesitatingly place us among the behaviorists. We acknowledge willingly our historical roots in the old behaviorism, but we do not accept the dead connotation of the label. We believe that all psychology is behavioristic or, better, that the category includes all psychologists who hold to a naturalistic view of their science. In addition, within present-day behaviorism, we find *reinforcement theory* most satisfactory. Finally, we think that reinforcement theory has been given its most useful and comprehensive exposition by B. F. Skinner in his major work, *The Behavior of Organisms.*

Our agreement in viewpoint led us to conclude that our own introductory course was to be biologically toned, experimentally grounded, and systematically presented. We decided to offer a theoretical organization of fact, explicitly and unashamedly, rejecting confusion in favor of order, secure in the knowledge that this is the whole aim of scientific endeavor. Our subject matter, behavior, was to be treated in terms of the variables of which it is a function and the lawful processes it reveals. The generality of our "general" course was to be in terms of basic principles underlying all behavior, however variegated or of whatever species. The major problems were to be treated under a few main headings: conditioning; extinction; generalization and discrimination; induction and differentiation; motivation; and, possibly, emotion.

With such an approach, topics like intelligence, personality, and thinking do not make up a course in general psychology. Instead, they are specialized fields in which basic principles work themselves out in complex fashion under the influence of a cumulative behavioral biography. Moreover, the study of the nervous system, of receptors and effectors, or of the organism's genetic endowment ("heredity" and "environment") does not figure in a course of this sort. These matters are left to advanced study or bequeathed, perhaps, in the division of scientific labor, to the physiologist and geneticist. They become areas of study for those who are interested in the intervening bodily factors which act as prerequisites or parameters for stimulus-response relations.

How to Teach. Our third line of thought was concerned with the *form* of the beginning course. Here our task was simpler. We concluded quickly that laboratory work must be an integral part of elementary instruction. The study of behavior is essentially an experimental science, and we felt that the value of a course of lectures, or lectures and demonstrations, would not alone be optimal. Laboratory work, we agreed, can make for a more mature understanding of a science and its methods. It is sounder pedagogically, permitting more active participation of the student in the educational process. It gives concreteness to the lecture material and a sense of proof and security about the facts that are learned. Besides, an experimental discipline needs laboratory preparation if advanced work is to be done. There could be no doubt, as we saw it, that our new course would profit by following our sister sciences in this respect.

With the goal, the content, and the form of our course clear in outline, we still had the practical part of our job ahead of us—the actual working out of our program. This presented a fresh set of questions, some of the answers to which are given, and others implied, in the account that follows.

The Course in Operation. A student taking introductory psychology at Columbia attends two one-hour lectures and four consecutive laboratory hours per week. The class meets as a whole for lectures and is subdivided into sections for laboratory. The course extends for one year (Psychology 1-2 in our bulletin) and admits students of sophomore standing or above. Because of the integrated sequence of work, the first half of the course is an absolute prerequisite for the second.

1. The lectures. Several problems arose in connection with the lecture material. One was the continual necessity for deciding what was elementary. Our systematic orientation answered the question of which major topics to cover, but did not tell us how far to pursue each one—at which stage the material became too advanced for the beginner. A second problem came from our need to expand certain theoretical points, deducing consequences when required, in order to fill in the picture we were trying to paint. A third was presented by our desire to offer some cautious extrapolations from experimental data (often obtained at the subhuman level) to human conduct in daily life. While stressing the complexity of the human case as compared with that of, say, the rat or chimpanzee, we still wished to supply instances of an everyday sort to which our basic principles might reasonably be said to apply. Our solutions of these problems cannot be given here, but anyone can see that our task was not easy.

A related problem came from our lack of a textbook suitable for use in connection with our lectures. In the first year of the course, we distributed mimeographed notes to our students. These served as an outline of the material covered, but their inadequacy was soon apparent. Reluctantly, in the second year, we decided to write our own text, and we managed to turn out, in installments, a rough draft which we sold to our class.

The major subdivisions of our lecture content, and of our text as planned, are as follows: Psychology and the Reflex; Respondent Conditioning; Operant Conditioning; Extinction and Reconditioning; Generalization and Discrimination; Differentiation; Chaining; Secondary Reinforcement; Motivation; Emotion; and Social Behavior. There is a logical sequence in this presentation which makes the later sections incomprehensible unless the earlier ones have been mastered. This gives a unified character to our product which is absent from the conventional course or text. If the titles and the order of treatment suggest a narrowness of outlook which is inconsistent with the wealth of data accessible to the present-day teacher, we can only point out that, within such a framework, it is possible to discuss reaction times, memorizing and forgetting, concept formation, meaning, insight, sensory and motor skills, pleasantness and unpleasantness, punishment, repression, regression, anxiety, and a number of other concepts in a way that takes little from their intrinsic interest or significance.

2. The Laboratory. Laboratory work, ideally, should be related, in content and time, to important aspects of the lecture and reading material. It was plain to us from the outset that our needs would be different from those of other laboratory courses in general psychology because of the difference in our course content. All signs pointed toward work with animals. We chose the white rat because it is hardy, inexpensive, convenient in size, easy to keep, and well suited to exemplify the principles we were to emphasize in our teaching. We were then faced with the task of preparing room facilities, selecting appropriate experiments, and constructing apparatus.

A large room was divided by partitions into sixteen cubicles arranged along three walls; they open upon a central area into which chairs could be moved during discussion periods. The fourth wall of the room holds a blackboard in front of which is a long instructor's desk or table. Each cubicle contains an apparatus table upon which is mounted a Dazor float-ing lamp fixture; two student chairs; and a shelf from which hang various lengths and colors of plug-in wire for electrical connections, and which holds a number of accessory items like cellophane tape, scissors, and a bottle of food pellets. Other supplies may be obtained on occasion from the instructor's desk or are distributed by assistants.

A full set of the major apparatus pieces in each cubicle includes: (1) a lever which the animal is conditioned to press, providing a behavior sample that is used in many of the experiments; (2) a food-magazine for auto-matic delivery of pellet-rewards; (3) a four-channel tape recorder for obtaining temporal relations between stimuli and responses; (4) a kymo-graph for obtaining cumulative response records of the animal's behavior; and (5) a stimulus-control box that acts as a power source and a means for regulating such stimuli as light and electric shock. From a signal generator on the instructor's table, a wire runs around the room and is connected with a speaker in each cubicle for presentation of auditory stimuli. Practically all of this apparatus, and a few other special pieces, was designed for our laboratory and built in our shop.[3] In addition, we have found especially useful a combined living-and-working cage for each experimental animal. This cage, in which the rat is housed at all times, alone makes large-scale work with rats possible. It eliminates all handling of animals by students or the caretaker, and reduces generally the emo-tional upset that often impedes progress and obscures experimental results.

At the semester's opening, each student is assigned a cage containing a freshly bought rat with which he works during the entire term. (A new animal is supplied for the second semester, when the old ones are donated to Columbia's Medical Center.) The caretaker of the departmental vivarium looks after the cleaning of cages, maintenance of feeding regi-mens, and the like. A laboratory fee of five dollars per student per term provides for the purchase and care of animals, as well as expendable laboratory supplies.

At the first laboratory meeting of a section, students are paired and cubicles assigned. At the same time, careful instruction is given in the operation and treatment of apparatus; information sheets are distributed; the writing of laboratory reports is discussed; and other arrangements are made for the experimental work that begins on the following week. A "dry run" is carried out, involving the hookup of apparatus, operation checks by instructor or assistant, and transportation of cages from vivarium to laboratory and back.

The second meeting, and each one thereafter, is begun with a "briefing" of the assembled section. In general, this briefing covers the following points: (1) purpose and procedure of the experiment; (2) significance of the experiment and its relation to lecture material; (3) apparatus hookup (a diagram is often made and left on the blackboard for reference); (4) treatment of the data collected; and (5) nature of the laboratory report desired. There is often lively discussion during this period, with students raising questions much more freely and informally than is possible at the lecture meetings. In addition to its reviewing and clarifying function, the briefing period permits some discussion of the design of experiments and proper use of experimental controls, the methods and rationale of simple descriptive and inferential statistics, and the like. An excellent opportunity to supplement the lectures is thereby exploited.

"Procedure sheets" are distributed to students during each briefing. They carry statements of the week's problem, the procedure to be used, the data to be gathered, and the treatment of data to be applied. They also contain questions (and space for answers) relevant to the work of the week and, sometimes, of preceding weeks. With questions answered and data appended, these sheets constitute the laboratory report. They are mimeographed on punched paper so that students may keep them in a loose-leaf binder and accumulate them to make up a manual of the year's work.

Briefings usually last about an hour. Then the students go to their cubicles to hook up their apparatus and otherwise prepare for the day's work. When a pair signals its readiness, the apparatus is examined by the instructor or assistant and tested for operation. When all cubicles have been checked, the cubicle lights are turned on, the room lights are turned off, and one member of each pair reports to the vivarium for his animal. Cubicle partners alternate in the order of working their animals in successive laboratory periods, and help one another in conducting each experiment. Whether, on a given day, the partners perform duplicate experiments or use a slight variation of procedure, the use of two animals gives a greater assurance of results and permits inter-animal comparison for variability. Total working time for the two animals is figured so as to allow an interval at the end of the period for writing reports, which are completed and handed in before the student leaves the laboratory. Graded and corrected reports are returned during the section's next laboratory meeting on the following week.

The entire introductory course is staffed by four instructors and four assistants, together with a reader who prepares and grades examinations. Each laboratory section is handled by an instructor and one assistant who do the briefing, get the section started on its work, and pass upon the laboratory reports. Instructors and assistants gather in weekly conferences to decide upon future experiments, to look after the writing of procedure sheets, to agree upon the general content of the briefings, to discuss class progress, to exchange impressions and recommendations, and so on.

All the experiments performed in the laboratory deal with operant or instrumental behavior. With four consecutive hours of laboratory work each week, and thirty weeks in the academic year, it is apparent that considerable ground can be covered. The first semester is occupied mainly with experiments of a fairly routine nature, the outcome of which, in each case, is well known to the instructor in advance. At the end of the term, two or three periods are given over to some novel project aimed at giving the student a feeling of fresh exploration. The second semester, which also closes with a class project, permits a wider choice of experiments throughout, more off the beaten track and at times a bit spectacular. Since an organism is a cumulator of its history, the experiments done within each semester must be carefully selected. Participation of an animal in one experiment must not be permitted to confound the results of another. In a few cases, it is necessary to counteract the influence of an earlier conditioning by subjecting the animal to an extinction period before setting him a new problem, but the proper sequence of experiments will greatly minimize this need. Moreover, the cross-comparison of results with animals that have different histories may be of interest in itself.

A partial list, by title, of the exepriments performed last year (1947-48) in our laboratory is given below. In some cases, an experiment required one period; in others, it was carried on for two, or even three periods without apparent exhaustion of its implications or loss of student appeal.

1. Operant conditioning with regular reinforcement.
2. Retention and extinction of a conditioned operant.
3. Periodic reconditioning (at fixed intervals).
4. The formation of a discrimination.
5. The reversal of a discrimination.
6. The effect of punishment.
7. The reduction of operant latency ("reaction time").
8. Chaining.
9. Secondary reinforcement.
10. The effect of drive upon response rate.
11. Light aversion.
12. Conditioning an avoidance response.
13. The conflict of motives.
14. An experimental prototype of "fetishism."
15. An experimental prototype of "masochism."

A fairly large number of students take introductory psychology at Columbia. Since each student has his own rat, the amount of data turned out each week is impressive. Despite the non-optimal conditions of experimentation, the trends of behavior revealed by so many animal groups may be useful in forecasting results to be expected from better controlled studies. We have, on occasion, had the class do the exploratory work required on some problem of more than instructional interest. The hearty cooperation of undergraduates is easily engaged and maintained for such work when they understand the significance of the problem and can see the progress they are making in its solution. We are convinced that such participation in the business of science makes for better education, whether as background for the liberal arts student or special training for the one who plans a scientific career.

An Evaluation. Although our introductory course now seems to us a natural, even conservative sort of thing, we know that, to some, it will seem radical. A few may applaud it; others may find some good in it; many, perhaps, will reject the whole conception as ill-advised or dangerous. In our opinion, we are trying out a new approach to psychological education. We think that a thoroughgoing reform is needed, and we are attempting to move in that direction. But we are not blind to the fact that our offering is only one of several that are possible today; and we feel that other attempts to reorganize instruction ought to be made by exponents of other theoretical views. Intelligent students are the same sharp listeners as our professional colleagues, even though not as well informed. In the best tradition of scientific scepticism, they will query and profane our most beloved dogmas. The struggle for survival of scientific theories is fought in many arenas and the victory must be won in all. It will not do to forget the classroom.

Available indications point to the general good health of our course, but we can see that it has weak points. A major defect arises from the fact that an overly large registration compels us to mass each student's laboratory hours on one day of the week. Originally, we planned on two two-hour periods per week, with students working singly rather than in pairs. Four consecutive hours of laboratory can become fatiguing. Moreover, the pairing of students, while not without advantages, sometimes leaves one partner with time on his hands. These are problems that can only be solved by increasing our facilities and the size of our staff.

Our class enrollment, in our first year of operation, was 120, twice the number we had expected. (There are about 1500-1800 students combined in the sophomore, junior and senior classes of Columbia College in any one year.) Last year it was 180 which is the maximum that present space and equipment can support. We had approximately 300 applications for this year, of whom only 180 could be accepted; and we have a list of about 30 men applying for places in the 1949-50 class. This congestion, which is embarrassing, has been increased to some extent by the fact that, last year, without petition from us, the College's committee on instruction voted to grant science credit to students who passed the course. Lacking additional laboratory facilities, we are in the unhappy position of being unable to accept more than three-fifths of our applicants.

Visitors to our laboratory often ask about the cost of setting up such a course. Actually, we spent about $5,500 for this purpose. As most science courses go, this is a pittance; for a laboratory course in psychology, it is a fairly large figure. We hasten to point out, however, that our course, being a *first*, was necessarily expensive. We had many problems of apparatus design and construction which, although now solved, went through several stages and entailed no small amount of labor and materials. Moreover, we aimed at the very best of equipment and facilities, looking toward durability under almost continual hard usage, and toward suitability not only for undergraduate instruction but for graduate research if desired. Although we tried to be frugal in our purchasing and to avoid hasty modifications or costly variation, we were often forced to spend more than we had planned upon. Today, we could reproduce nearly every piece of apparatus at a fraction of its original cost. Furthermore, there is nothing that we use which could not, in the interests of economy alone, be greatly simplified or even eliminated. The feeding of animals during experimentation could be done by hand rather than electrically; satisfactory cumulative response curves could be plotted with a pencil on a piece of graph paper; timing could be done with an ordinary watch; living-working cages could be made of wire mesh and wood; response levers could be made from metal coat hangers or similar material; and so on. Large cubicles could be done away with in favor of banks of compartments like those described by Carl Pfaffmann.[4] Even the cost of animals could be reduced by dispensing with institute-bred rats and using such an animal as the pigeon which can be trapped on almost any campus and makes an excellent experimental subject. In fact, our course could be copied *in toto* for less money than it now takes most teachers to set up the simplest kind of introduction to experimental psychology.

We are frequently asked another question, of a very different sort: Aren't your students handicapped for advanced work by the kind of course that you give them? This cannot be answered in a sentence. As far as advanced work in Columbia College is concerned, we can give a clear *No*, since our first course is basic to nearly all the others in our department. With respect to students who transfer to other colleges and take up advanced work, we have few reports, but they are in agreement. Such students tell us that they encounter no serious difficulties and feel that no 'restriction' was imposed by their work with us; they express strong approval of what we did with them in their first course. We are pleased, but not surprised, at such reactions. Despite many deletions of material covered in the usual introductory course, we have retained much of the 'classical' content. In addition, we feel that our students have had advantages not ordinarily provided: they know scientific work at first hand; they can appreciate good data and criticize bad; and they are sophisticated about the ordering of facts. In advanced work, they should be able to learn what is required of them; their confusion, where it exists, should be no greater than that of their fellows; and where new material has no ties with *any* theoretical viewpoint, they can hardly have been impaired by us. As for those students who move on to graduate study at Columbia or elsewhere, we have no reason, on the basis of Graduate Record Examinations, course grades, or personal reports, to believe them hampered by, or lacking in, undergraduate background. Finally, of the men who "take but one course" in psychology, we can only express our belief, implicit throughout this paper, that a sound knowledge of a few basic principles of behavior is a greater gift from us than anything else we could provide.

Looking back, we feel that we have done, as well as we could, what we thought was needed. Whether it can be done better, or deserves to be done at all, we leave for the future to show.

The Advanced Courses. As mentioned at the beginning of this report, our early discussions were not concerned exclusively with the introductory offering. We saw our reorganization as extending ultimately throughout the undergraduate curriculum. This extension depended, however, upon the success of the first course—our only innovation in 1946-47. This course having gone well from the start, four new courses were introduced in the following year. Two of them, Discrimination and Motivation, were laboratory courses; and two of them were seminars. This year, another laboratory course, in Conditioning, is being added. All of these are one-term courses, taught by the regular staff with the aid of two additional laboratory assistants. Three lecture courses of our old curriculum were retained: Abnormal, Social, and Differential Psychology. Of these, only the Abnormal has undergone a revision in line with reinforcement theory. The other two, although not at odds with this viewpoint, do not depend so clearly upon the first-course material and will not be discussed in the present context.

The course in Discrimination (Psychology 3 in our bulletin) has two lectures and two three-hour laboratory periods per week. The subject matter, as indicated by the title, is a further study of discriminative processes and capacities, along representative lines. Like the other advanced laboratory courses, it is handled by one instructor and one assistant, and a laboratory fee of $5.00 is charged each student.

Before 1947-48, we had for years offered a two-semester sequence called "experimental psychology" which was, as in many other colleges, our only laboratory course. This practice, in the light of our discussions, came to look strange, implying as it did that experimental psychology was a topic rather than a set of methods, and that here alone a student could learn the experimental side of an experimental science. We could imagine, as a parallel, a chemistry department that offered a single course in "experimental chemistry." Moreover, our beginning course was equally experimental, and it was our desire to provide laboratory work in as many of our courses as possible. Consequently, we dropped the old designation and substituted two new courses, entitling these simply "Discrimination" and "Motivation" to describe their topical content. Of these two, the former most closely approximates the old "Experimental," at least in the repertory of experiments and the use of human subjects. The experiments performed in the class last year included: the formation of a time discrimination; visual acuity; reaction time; dark adaptation; phase and time differences in auditory localization; contour graphs for apparent weights and apparent lengths; and concept formation.

Psychology 4, the *Motivation* course, also consists of two lecture hours and six laboratory hours, as in the case of Discrimination. All experiments to date have been done with white rats, fresh animals being supplied for each new experimental unit. A new, small-scale laboratory was constructed for this course and several new pieces of apparatus were added to the basic battery used in Psychology 1-2. The course is addressed to a further study of motivation—its types and properties. Last year's experiments included: the effect of motivational level at the time of conditioning and extinction; discriminative stimulus accompaniments of motivation; anxiety and avoidance behavior; and several studies of the transferability of secondary reinforcement. We found that a laboratory course in this area is entirely feasible. Many motives (hunger, thirst, light-aversion, anxiety, etc.) are accessible; other operants than lever-pressing may be employed (e.g., cage-crossing, chain-pulling, and panel-pushing); and published experiments may be repeated or new ones designed.

Psychology 5, our *Abnormal Psychology,* is at present a three-point lecture course. Classical material is covered, but emphasis is placed upon recent experimental findings and an attempt is made to organize the facts within reinforcement theory. We hope that, within a year or two, this course may be made into a laboratory course, after the pattern of Psychology 3, 4, and 6. There is available in the present-day literature of this field a number of experiments, both animal and human, which could easily serve as a starting point for such an offering.

Psychology 6, *Conditioning,* is to be given for the first time in the Spring Session of 1948-49. It too will be a laboratory course, utilizing the facilities of Psychology 4, and dealing exclusively with problems of operant conditioning in the white rat. A final selection of this year's experiments has not yet been made.

Psychology 15 and 16 are two seminars in *Contemporary Research Problems*. Each meets for two consecutive hours a week. Registration is limited in number, and only those students who have had training in several courses are admitted. The catalog description of each course reads: "Through readings, reports, and discussions, central problems of present-day psychology are considered and experimental designs for research are formulated. The general topic for this session is . . . ." Last year, when these seminars were given for the first time, the topic for Psychology 15 was *verbal behavior;* for Psychology 16, *emotion.* Neither seminar is prerequisite for the other and a student may enroll in either or both. Senior psychology 'majors' are given priority, and each seminar is attended by the same four instructors who had charge of Psychology 1-2—a device that has been profitable for staff as well as students.

Concluding Remarks. Our undergraduate curriculum is, then, almost entirely integrated into a cohesive sequence. The principles developed in the first course sound the keynote and are a real prerequisite for all but two of the advanced offerings. The overlap between the introductory and advanced courses has been sharply reduced, if not eleminated altogether. The laboratory and the seminar have displaced or supplemented the lecture wherever and whenever we have found it possible. Use of animal subjects in the laboratories has been made without apology whenever it appeared that fundamentals of behavior would thereby be more readily grasped, but extrapolations from the rat to man have always been made with due caution. Yet basic problems of human behavior have been the ultimate concern of our teaching.

Such a curriculum as we have achieved was in no sense a private feat, nor was it built *in vacuo.* A spearhead must have its shaft, and we are gratefully aware that the execution of our plan depended upon many persons and circumstances. An indispensable condition was the conjuncture, at one institution and at one time, of individuals who functioned as a team. We, and those who shared with us the day-to-day problems, had a common theoretical leaning and similar scientific aims. Within our group were men and women of varied and complementary talents, together with a spirit of selfless cooperation that permitted each one to make his maximal contribution to the common cause.

Finally, to our departmental colleagues and the Columbia College administrators we owe many thanks. From them we received a free hand and the generous means to try out our idea. To our voiced needs and unspoken hopes, they responded with warm encouragement and material support. Even when they did not see eye to eye with us, they were willing, with courageous and objective interest, to give us their trust and confidence in testing out a program.

Notes

1. Henry E. Garrett, late Professor Emeritus of Psychology at Columbia, and a Visiting Professor in Education at the University of Virginia after 1956, was later to be Chairman of our Department and responsible for much of my own advance within it.

2. See Dael Wolfle's article in the *American Psychologist,* 1947, *2,* 437-445.

3. For the design and construction of apparatus, we are especially indebted to John Volkmann, F. L. Blendinger, and F. C. Frick, without whose combined enthusiasm and talents we certainly could not have launched our program as soon or as adequately as we did. Dr. Frick, who was (with Dr. D. H. Bullock) an assistant during the first year of the course, has taken the principal part in writing up some notes on our early apparatus models (*American Journal of Psychology,* 1948, *61,* 409-414).

4. See the *American Psychologist,* 1947, *2,* 559-560.

7

Order *versus* Confusion in the First Course

Our new curriculum at Columbia College excited considerable comment. Some of our colleagues, like Professors Yerkes, Muenzinger, and Hull, wrote enthusiastic letters of approval, especially of our introductory course. Others, like Professor Wendt, were negative in their appraisals. The Freudians at Columbia attacked us to a man, although we simply offered a fresh interpretation of their concepts. Eclectics, of course, remained eclectics, and the rest of the world was indifferent. Our curriculum as a whole has seldom been adopted since, although parts of it are widely taught and animal experiments are a common feature of modern undergraduate laboratory teaching.

In 1953, I took part in a symposium on *Goals of the First Course in Psychology,* at the 61st annual meeting of The American Psychology Association, in Cleveland, Ohio. The following paper, delivered on September 5th, was my contribution.

The "order" and "confusion" in my title refer to the teaching situation in our introductory psychology course during two seven-year periods at Columbia College. I have used *confusion* to describe our introductory course during the period from 1939 to 1946; and *order* to describe it between 1946 and 1953.

There was nothing unique about our course during the first of these two periods, either in content or in manner of presentation. Our approach could well have been called *eclectic,* in that the content was borrowed freely from a variety of sources, but it was permeated by a strong flavor of objectivism. It was *catholic,* too, in that we tried to be of interest to everyone.

We used such standard texts as those of Woodworth, Murphy, Ruch, and Boring, Langfeld, and Weld. Our lectures were sprinkled with the customary references to ancient and medieval thinkers, to the British empiricists, to the nineteenth century physiologists, and to such pioneers as Wundt, James, Ebbinghaus, and Binet. We had something to say about the history of psychology, and a little more to say about the schools. We covered most of the standard topics—from Methods and Measures through Sensing, Perceiving, and Learning to Feeling, Emotion, Motivation, and Personality. We added something about the Response Mechanism, Individual Differences, Abnormality, and What-Psychology-Is-Not. We provided classroom demonstrations of such things as Visual Phi, Mnemonic Systems, Intelligence Testing, Stylus-Maze Learning, Lie Detection, and Ideo-Motor Action. We tested our students twice or more per term to find out if they knew that *closure* was a Gestalt concept, Fechner was a psychophysicist, IQ = MA/CA x 100, and Falstaff was markedly *endomorphic.*

This was a period of inconsistency and disorder, but it didn't bother us much at first. Our lectures were not often interrupted with questions, and awkward situations seldom arose, in class or out. No one asked how *memory* was related to *conditioning,* how *conditioning* was related to *concept formation,* how *concept formation* was related to *discrimination,* or how *discrimination* was related to *association by similarity.* No one, including the teacher, thought much about such matters. We moved rapidly from topic to topic or chapter to chapter, in any order that we chose, since there was not much reason to think of one as more basic than another or more essential to its comprehension. We skated over all the thin ice at high speed; we emphasized the dramatic instance and the surprising result; and we saved our most interesting material for the last part of the course.

Awareness of our confusion came about gradually during this period. It arose as we began to understand the import of modern behavior theory and permitted it to creep into our lectures. Beginning with a toehold in the realm of conditioning, this systematic development soon contained our treatments of learning, memory, forgetting, and problem solving. Then it worked into our discussion of emotion and motivation, of language development, and even discrimination. Ultimately it threatened to swallow up or push aside most of the earlier content of our course.

It became obvious that the bulk of our lecturing was at odds with either the concepts, the arrangement, or the interpretations provided by our textbooks and collateral readings. Confusion reached its peak; everyone was unhappy, including our students; and some resolution had to be found.

There were several alternatives: (1) We might spend more time in the attempt to iron out differences between teacher and text. (2) We might throw examination emphasis upon *either* the lectures *or* the reading, treating the other as a kind of informational bonus or an unavoidable form of extra duty that was not to be taken very seriously. (3) We might set aside our systematic bias, follow our text closely, and gloss over any internal inconsistencies that appeared. (4) We might beg off from teaching the first course and avoid the problem altogether. (Fortunate is the man who can do this!) (5) We might write a textbook of our own, hoping that our new integration would still find room for most of the factual data in the conventional approach.

We chose the fifth alternative. We undertook to write our own text, and we reorganized our first course in accordance with the fresh design. We reduced our weekly lectures from three to two and added a four-hour laboratory-and-discussion section. Using the white rat as our principal laboratory subject, we were able to set up a series of experiments which illustrated all but one or two of the central teachings of our lectures and our text. We committed ourselves wholeheartedly to system, and endeavored to extend it to its limits at the first-course level.

At the outset our offering was thin. We felt the absence of some of the material we had pushed aside in the interests of order and system. Big holes were left where there had been sections on sense-organ and nervous-system structure and function; on history and schools of psychology; on individual differences and abnormalities; and on personality studies. Moreover, we were animal-bound and too close to our own special interests in research. This gave an impression of narrowness and prejudice that was not entirely unwarranted. It required time and, especially, the completion of our textbook to correct these faults. Gradually, however, more and more human studies and references came into our lectures, and other-than-rat experiments appeared in our laboratory sequence. Today we are able to incorporate as many and as great a variety of items as we were in the old days, but these items are now an integral part of a meaningful whole.

After seven years of teaching from a systematic viewpoint, we can compare our present setup rather unemotionally with the older one, pointing up some of the advantages and disadvantages for the teacher and the pupil. Let's begin with the latter who is, as we often say, the all-important one.

Following their exposure to the conventional type of first course, our students were probably as well qualified as most to go on to other courses and for discussion of psychology with their peers. They were familiar with many names and many facts, at least at the time they took their final examination. They knew a little about a great many problems, methods, and theories, and they were fairly critical in their evaluation of new ideas. They were at ease in the presence of psychology students from other colleges; they had no difficulty with the psychological articles in *Time* or the *Ladies' Home Journal*; and they were equally at home with the relevant material in the movies and on the radio.

Moreover, they were quite satisfied with their first course. They ranked it well in the yearly popularity poll, and complaints about its content were infrequent. Only during the last part of our first period, when our own dissatisfaction was greatest, did any appreciable number of students mention our inconsistencies or disagreements. Apparently students do not ask much of their beginning course in psychology.

A different picture is presented by our more recent product. This student comes out with a fairly clear understanding of a few things—conditioning, extinction, generalization, discrimination, response differentiation, and chaining, as well as primary and secondary reinforcement, both positive and negative. He may use these terms appropriately and with facility, in his writing and discussions. He may be able to cite some of the research data connected with each concept. In the optimal case he may be able to apply his knowledge to practical problems and everyday matters with some success. He may also have something to say about the relation of his principles to the analysis of such things as concept formation, delayed reaction, intelligence, insight, the Rorschach test, transfer of training, secondary drives, and psychoanalysis.

On the other hand he will lack acquaintance with numerous facts and interpretations that the conventionally trained student possesses. He may know nothing of the Zeigarnik effect, the Szondi test, or the Zoellner illusion; the relation of birth order to intelligence; the purpose of a pseudophone or a color perimeter; the problem of test reliability; the function of the endocrine glands; or even the anatomy of the neuron. He is therefore likely to be upset when he comes into contact with students who have the broader orientation; he has difficulty in understanding and in being understood. He often has a strong suspicion that his teachers were too narrow and that his training was defective. Things may adjust themselves in time, but he will not soon lose the feeling that there are more things to account for in the world of behavior than he had ever surmised!

There are also *pros* and *cons* from the teacher's point of view. On the positive side we have found greater satisfaction in our classroom work and in our student contacts elsewhere. We are no longer annoyed by having to deal with areas of content in which we have no vital interest or in which we have limited or inadequate information. Each basic element of our course is as attractive as the next in developing the final picture.

Also, as we develop the principal features of our position, we often find that our better students are not only well abreast of our exposition, but are actually in advance of it, to the point of anticipating topics to be considered and questions to be raised. Our lectures are no longer merely lectures; they contain a large amount of give and take. We have found it profitable to encourage this student participation, even when it amounted to hostile expression. This is especially the case in our laboratory sections, where we have occasionally gone so far as to instigate "gripe sessions," to improve morale and acquaint ourselves with some of our deficiencies.

We are happier about examinations under the new order. We no longer lean upon so much rote memorizing of proper names and small items of fact, theory, or method. We stress instead the analysis of problems, the design of experiments, and the application of principles. "Thought questions" now dominate our quizzes and exams, especially in the second term. These questions give rise to plenty of discussion, but they are seldom charged with being trivial.

The staff of our first course normally consists of three or four instructors and as many assistants. In the old days they might have provided six or eight different answers to some student's question. In a systematic course, the answers are obviously more uniform and we are very rarely badgered by the complaint that we 'ought to get together.' Of course our answers may be alike and still be wrong, but a united front has its agreeable aspects!

An additional satisfaction is derived from the fact that our present course attracts a much greater proportion of high-grade science students than did the old one. We have not drawn large numbers to our advanced courses, but we have, since 1946, sent more than 30 Columbia College students into graduate work in psychology at various universities. This is to be compared with *two* in the earlier period.

There is also a negative side to our picture, from the teacher's point of view. If he is more successful in attracting high-grade students, he is probably less successful with the below-average group in a systematic course.

The student who gets off to a bad start or falls behind the rest of the class in a conventional course is still able to turn over a new leaf and improve his performance in the next section of the course, almost irrespective of what has gone before. In our present course, where mastery at one stage depends upon mastery at the preceding stage, this is not so easily done. It is my impression, lacking data, that we lose a larger percentage of our students than we used to. It may be, of course, that the ones we lose are merely more *noticeable* in their failure to talk our language than they were in the old days.

The teacher of a systematic course cannot but be disturbed by some of his pupils' resentment of *indoctrination*. The teacher, himself, has had to decide for or against system, and he is not always sure that he has acted for the best. When an able, hard-working student complains about the course's lack of breadth, the teacher cannot avoid an occasional qualm. When teaching an eclectic course, he may have had complaints about the lack of system, but *this* complaint is here and now. Besides, he cannot point, as he might have before, to many colleagues who take the same position.

This raises a final point. The teacher of a systematic approach to psychology is almost certain to get adverse criticism, at first, second, or third hand, from psychologists with eclectic leanings. He is bound to feel a degree of isolation from the members of his profession. He will often wonder if he isn't too eccentric, bigoted, or imbecilic to see the folly of his ways. He will worry about the correspondent who suggests that he is cheating his pupils of their rightful heritage at Columbia. He will be disturbed by the public letter that accuses him of cultism and prays that others will not follow in his path. He will cherish overmuch any expression of encouragement and commendation; and he will take particular pleasure in the following quotation from a once-authoritative figure.[1]

Psychology . . . has only recently turned to scientific methods; and when the time came for it to take its place among the sciences, there was naturally difference of opinion regarding the standpoint it should assume, the procedure it should follow, the model it should seek to copy. Where such differences of opinion obtain, the best way to begin your study is to *master one system thoroughly;* your ideas are thus made consistent and your knowledge receives an orderly arrangement; then, as you read further, you can use this system as a touchstone whereby to test new ideas and to arrange new knowledge; and if the new ideas seem preferable to the old, or if the old framework breaks down under the new knowledge, you can alter your system accordingly. If you begin, on the contrary, by studying

97

a number of works abreast, you are liable to become confused. And it is better to be wrong than to be muddled; for truth, as Bacon said, emerges more quickly from error than from confusion.

Notes

1. Titchener, E. B. *A Beginner's Psychology*. New York: The Macmillan Company, 1915.

8

A Personal Course
in Psychology

This paper was read at the 71st Meeting of the American Psychological Association, in Philadelphia, Pennsylvania, on August 31st, 1963. It was later published in a collection of papers on *The Control of Behavior,* edited by R. Ulrich, T. Stachnik, and J. Mabry, and published by Scott, Foresman, and Company in 1966. Its background will be described in some detail in a summarizing paper, *An International Venture in Behavior Modification* (see page 131).

This paper is reprinted from *The Control of Behavior,* edited by R. Ulrich, T. Stachnik, and J. Mabry, Scott, Foresman, and Company. It is reprinted with permission from Scott, Foresman, and Company.

I would like you to imagine that you have recently agreed to help establish a department of psychology. It is to be complete in every respect, with all the major specializations and at every level of training from the first course to the most advanced, in a university that is just being formed, and in a country where no such department now exists. Together with four young psychologists and former pupils as co-workers, you are expected to take a constructive part in procuring a complete staff, purchasing equipment, outfitting a library, designing a department building and, especially, developing a curriculum of study. You have been assured of financial and moral support, and you have been told to be as bold and experimental as you wish in the program you adopt.

Imagine, too, that in a few months you will have awaiting you, at the university's opening, a group of perhaps 100 students, fairly well grounded in language, mathematics, arts, and other sciences, who want basic psychological training. You and your colleagues, with a few assistants, working in temporary quarters and with limited facilities, are expected to introduce them to psychology and to carry them thereafter as far as they may want to go.

To start you on your way, you and your colleagues have spent a month or more in visiting colleges, universities, hospitals, and research centers where psychology is taught in one way or another. You have talked with interested teachers and researchers about your problem; you have examined shops, laboratories, libraries, classrooms, and clinics. You have taken notes on everything and tried to extract from every experience something of value for your project. You have bought books and ordered equipment. And you have sat down together at the end of your travels to decide on your next objective. What is it going to be?

Under such conditions I suggest that your first concern would be the introductory course and those 100-odd students who will be enrolled therein. There is only *one* introductory course and it is, or should be, a key course and a foundation for work to come. While teaching it, you and your co-workers can prepare for the courses that immediately follow. At the same time, you can begin your search for a distinguished staff of teachers at the more advanced levels. These new teachers will, in turn, help you design and equip your workshops and laboratories, stock your library, give form and clearer purpose to your program and, finally, help you to design your building. Right now your job is to get ready for those 100 young men and women who will be there to greet you when the school bell rings.

But what sort of first course will you teach? There's much talk today about an educational reawakening; much dissatisfaction throughout this country with our aims, our methods, and the results we now achieve. Will you try to export a course that is under fire at home? Perhaps you, yourself, have complained about the failure of your teaching—talked about the inefficiency of the lecture system, the evil of examinations, the meaninglessness of letter and number grades, the short-term retention of course content, and the rigid frame of hours, days, and weeks within which each course of study is presumed to fit. Perhaps you have even expressed a willingness to change these things, if you could only escape from the "system." Now you have your chance. What are you going to do?

The kind of course I'm going to suggest has never been taught. It won't work. It conflicts with the natural tendencies of man. It has nothing new about it. Even if it worked, it could only teach reinforcement theory. It might be all right somewhere else, but it won't go here. And I think you will find, in the last analysis, that it is against the law. So, having anticipated some of your objections, let me tell you more about it.

It is a course with lectures, demonstraions, discussions, laboratory hours, and "home work." The lectures and demonstrations are infrequent and primarily inspirational. Ideally, they are interesting, informative, and memorable, even entertaining. Once the course has started, they are provided at suitable places along the way, but only for those students who have reached a point that guarantees an appreciation of their content. For students who do not qualify until a later date, a recording of the lecture and, if possible, the demonstration, is available. Attendance at either lectures or demonstrations, however, is entirely optional, and no examination is based upon them.

Discussions with one's peers or with an instructor, or both, are provided at certain times for those students who desire them and, as in the case of lectures and demonstrations, if they have earned the privilege. These discussions are also recorded and may be listened to again by any of the participants. Needless to say, the discussions are never to be used as examining devices by the teacher. They are primarily for the student, who has won the right to ask questions or to express himself with respect to the work he has been doing in the laboratory or at home.

The laboratory work itself begins on the second or third day of the course, and is its most important feature. Each student has his own private and well-equipped little room or cubicle, for a certain period of time each day—say an hour and a half—on five or six days of the week. There he works alone or, perhaps, with a partner, under the general supervision of a laboratory assistant who has no more than nine other students in his charge at the time. The student's daily task begins when he has qualified for it—for example, when he has turned in a report of the preceding day's experiment, answered two or three questions on the last reading assignment, studied a description of his laboratory mission for the day, or done all of these things.

The experiments themselves are carefully planned to let each student discover for himself the operation of certain well-established principles of behavior; to teach him some basic skills in the use of equipment and the treatment of data; and to lead him from minimal to maximal responsibility in the writing of reports.

When a laboratory task has been completed, and *only* then, the student receives the assignment that will prepare him for the next. This is his "home work." It may include textbook study, plain or programmed; the reading of an article or technical report, carefully edited or supplemented to make it fully clear, and provided with a few key questions like those he may be asked at the beginning of his next laboratory session; and other readings may be given solely as a reward for work completed and to whet the appetite for more.

Besides preparing him for further laboratory missions, lectures, demonstrations, and conferences, this work is intended to broaden the student's perspective by teaching him to generalize from the laboratory to many other situations of human life. It aims to encourage thinking in the direction of both research and practical application. And, finally, it is meant to provide the student with at least a nodding acquaintance with the great variety that goes by the name of psychology today.

The assistant's functions in such a course are very important. He is the one who prepares and checks equipment, collects reports, passes out work material and assignments, and records in each individual student's logbook each important step along the route, including the time of arrival and the number of setbacks, if any, before reaching port. He will also collect any student complaints, requests, comments, or suggestions (in writing), which he then passes on to the course director or other designated person.

The teachers, in a course like this, are not as conspicuous as they were under the old order. Their workload and responsibility, however, are as great as before, especially during the first year's operation. They are the ones who design, in every minute detail and initially for just one student, each day's teaching program; and they are the ones who redesign this program in the light of student performance and assistants' reports. They must also stand ready to give an occasional lecture or preside at a demonstration; they must sometimes be available for conference or discussion with qualified students; and they must be prepared to read an occasional student paper. Their general loss in visibility to their pupils, which might be aversive to longtime performers on the classroom stage, is perhaps offset by the improved reception of their messages when given and, more generally, the increased status of their academic position.

When all the course requirements have been met, the course is at an end. At this point the student's logbook is examined by the course director, who records the achievement, places the book in the department files, and takes a few moments, perhaps, to offer his congratulations. No final examination is given, no course grade, no reward for speed of attainment, and no punishment for delay. Examining and teaching were inseparable parts of the same educational process, and something better than a letter grade is available in a list of goals that were reached and the time it took to reach them. The student is ready for Course Number 2, a new logbook, a new cubicle, a new assistant, a new body of facts and skills, and, probably, a new teacher. But this is not, at the moment, our concern.

I have sketched for you a more or less imaginary first course in psychology, and I have suggested its more or less imaginary origin. More or less. Pilot research in this kind of teaching is already going on at several places in this country, although not exclusively aimed at first-course needs; and a full-scale test is now being planned for the first course itself, along the lines I have suggested here, at the new University of Brasilia, in Brazil, in 1964. If success attends these ventures, it might well be that some such personal-course method of instruction could be applied in other sciences and at other levels of education.

9

"Good-bye, teacher..."

The most popular paper I ever wrote was this one. It has been reprinted so many times that I wouldn't include it here if it weren't a kind of culmination of the story told by the others in this book. The paper was delivered at the 75th annual meeting of the American Psychological Association in Washington, D.C. (September 1967) to the members of Division 2, at the invitation of Neil R. Bartlett, then President of the Division.

This paper is reprinted from the *Journal of Applied Behavior Analysis*, 1968, *1*, 79-89. It is reprinted with permission from the *Journal of Applied Behavior Analysis*.

When I was a boy, and school "let out" for the summer, we used to celebrate our freedom from educational control by chanting:

Good-bye scholars, good-bye school;
Good-bye teacher, darned old fool!

We really didn't think of our teacher as deficient in judgment, or as a clown or jester. We were simply escaping from restraint, dinner pail in one hand and shoes in the other, with all the delights of summer before us. At that moment, we might even have been well-disposed toward our teacher and might have felt a touch of compassion as we completed the rhyme.

"Teacher" was usually a woman, not always young and not always pretty. She was frequently demanding and sometimes sharp of tongue, ever ready to pounce when we got out of line. But, occasionally, if one did especially well in homework or in recitation, he could detect a flicker of approval or affection that made the hour in class worthwhile. At such times, we loved our teacher and felt that school was fun.

It was not fun enough, however, to keep me there when I grew older. Then I turned to another kind of education, in which the reinforcements were sometimes just as scarce as in the schoolroom. I became a Western Union messenger boy and, between deliveries of telegrams, I learned Morse code by memorizing dots and dashes from a sheet of paper and listening to a relay on the wall. As I look back on those days, I conclude that I am the only living reinforcement theorist who ever learned Morse code in the absence of reinforcement.

It was a long, frustrating job. It taught me that dropout learning could be just as difficult as in-school learning and it led me to wonder about easier possible ways of mastering a skill. Years later, after returning to school and finishing my formal education, I came back to this classical learning problem, with the aim of making International Morse code less painful for beginners than American Morse had been for me (Keller, 1943).

During World War II, with the aid of a number of students and colleagues, I tried to apply the principle of immediate reinforcement to the early training of Signal Corps personnel in the reception of Morse-code signals. At the same time, I had a chance to observe, at close hand and for many months, the operation of a military training center. I learned something from both experiences, but I should have learned more. I should have seen many things that I didn't see at all, or saw very dimly.

I could have noted, for example, that instruction in such a center was highly individualized, in spite of large classes, sometimes permitting students to advance at their own speed throughout a course of study. I could have seen the clear specification of terminal skills for each course, together with the carefully graded steps leading to this end. I could have seen the demand for perfection at every level of training and for every student; the employment of classroom instructors who were little more than the successful graduates of earlier classes; the minimizing of the lecture as a teaching device and the maximizing of student participation. I could have seen, especially, an interesting division of labor in the educational process, wherein the noncommissioned classroom teacher was restricted to duties of guiding, clarifying, demonstrating, testing, grading, and the like, while the commissioned teacher, the training officer, dealt with matters of course logistics, the interpretation of training manuals, the construction of lesson plans and guides, the evaluation of student progress, the selection of noncommissioned cadre, and the writing of reports for his superiors.

I did see these things, of course, in a sense, but they were embedded deeply within a special context, one of "training" rather than "education." I did not then appreciate that a set of reinforcement contingencies which were useful in building simple skills like those of the radio operator might also be useful in developing the verbal repertories, the conceptual behaviors, and the laboratory techniques of university education. It was not until a long time later, by a very different route, that I came to such a realization.

That story began in 1962, with the attempt on the part of two Brazilian and two North American psychologists, to establish a Department of Psychology at the University of Brasilia. The question of teaching method arose from the very practical problem of getting a first course ready by a certain date for a certain number of students in the new university. We had almost complete freedom of action; we were dissatisfied with the conventional approaches; and we knew something about programmed instruction. We were also of the same theoretical persuasion. It was quite natural, I suppose, that we should look for fresh applications of reinforcement thinking to the teaching process (Keller, 1966).

The method that resulted from this collaborative effort was first used in a short-term laboratory course[1] at Columbia University in the winter of 1963, and the basic procedure of this pilot study was employed at Brasilia during the following year, by Professors Rodolfo Azzi and Carolina Martuscelli Bori, with 50 students in a one-term introductory course. Professor Azzi's report on this, at the 1965 meetings of the American Psychological Association and in personal correspondence, indicated a highly satisfactory outcome. The new procedure was received enthusiastically by the students and by the university administration. Mastery of the course material was judged excellent for all who completed the course. Objections were minor, centering around the relative absence of opportunity for discussion between students and staff.

Unfortunately, the Brasilia venture came to an abrupt end during the second semester of its operation, due to a general upheaval within the university that involved the resignation or dismissal of more than 200 teachers. Members of the original psychology staff have since taken positions elsewhere, and have reportedly begun to use the new method again, but I am unable at this time to report in detail on their efforts.

Concurrently with the early Brazilian development, Professor J. G. Sherman and I, in the spring of 1965, began a series of more or less independent applications of the same general method at Arizona State University. With various minor changes, this work has now been tried through five semesters with an increasing number of students per term (Keller, 1967b; Sherman, 1967). The results have been more gratifying with each successive class, and there has been as yet no thought of a return to more conventional procedures. In addition, we have had the satisfaction of seeing our system used by a few other colleagues in other courses and at other institutions.[2]

In describing this method to you, I will start with a quotation. It is from a handout given to all the students enrolled in the first-semester course in General Psychology (one of two introductions offered at Arizona State University) during the past year, and it describes the teaching method to which they will be exposed unless they elect to withdraw from the course.

"This is a course through which you may move, from start to finish, at your own pace. You will not be held back by other students or forced to go ahead until you are ready. At best, you may meet all the course requirements in less than one semester; at worse, you may not complete the job within that time. How fast you go is up to you.

"The work of this course will be divided into 30 units of content, which correspond roughly to a series of homework assignments and laboratory exercises. These units will come in a definite numerical order, and you must show your mastery of each unit (by passing a "readiness" test or carrying out an experiment) before moving on to the next.

"A good share of your reading for this course may be done in the classroom, at those times when no lectures, demonstrations, or other activities are taking place. Your classroom, that is, will sometimes be a study hall.

"The lectures and demonstrations in this course will have a different relation to the rest of your work than is usually the rule. They will be provided only when you have demonstrated your readiness to appreciate them; no examination will be based upon them; and you need not attend them if you do not wish. When a certain percentage of the class has reached a certain point in the course, a lecture or demonstration will be available at a stated time, but it will not be compulsory.

"The teaching staff of your course will include proctors, assistants, and an instructor. A proctor is an undergraduate who has been chosen for his mastery of the course content and orientation, for his maturity of judgment, for his understanding of the special problems that confront you as a beginner, and for his willingness to assist. He will provide you with all your study materials except your textbooks. He will pass upon your readiness tests as satisfactory or unsatisfactory. His judgment will ordinarily be law, but if he is ever in serious doubt, he can appeal to the classroom assistant, or even the instructor, for a ruling. Failure to pass a test on the first try, the second, the third, or even later, will not be held against you. It is better that you get too much testing than not enough, if your final success in the course is to be assured.

"Your work in the laboratory will be carried out under the direct supervision of a graduate laboratory assistant, whose detailed duties cannot be listed here. There will also be a graduate classroom assistant, upon whom your proctor will depend for various course materials (assignments, study questions, special readings, and so on), and who will keep up to date all progress records for course members. The classroom assistant will confer with the instructor daily, aid the proctors on occasion, and act in a variety of ways to further the smooth operation of the course machinery.

"The instructor will have as his principal responsibilities: (a) the selection of all study material used in the course; (b) the organization and the mode of presenting this material; (c) the construction of tests and examinations; and (d) the final evaluation of each student's progress. It will be his duty, also, to provide lectures, demonstrations, and discussion opportunities for all students who have earned the privilege; to act as a clearinghouse for requests and complaints; and to arbitrate in any case of disagreement between students and proctors or assistants. . . .

"All students in the course are expected to take a final examination, in which the entire term's work will be represented. With certain exceptions, this examination will come at the same time for all students, at the end of the term. . . . The examination will consist of questions which, in large part, you have already answered on your readiness tests. Twenty-five percent of your course grade will be based on this examination; the remaining 75 percent will be based on the number of units of reading and laboratory work that you have successfully completed during the term."

(In my own sections of the course, these percentages were altered, during the last term, to a 30 percent weighting of the final examination, a 20 percent weighting of the 10 laboratory exercises, and a 50 percent weighting of the reading units.)

A picture of the way this method operates can best be obtained, perhaps, by sampling the activities of a hypothetical average student as he moves through the course. John Pilgrim is a freshman, drawn from the upper 75 percent of his high-school class. He has enrolled in PY 112 for unknown reasons and has been assigned to a section of about 100 students, men and women, most of whom are also in their beginning year. The class is scheduled to meet on Tuesdays and Thursdays, from 9:15 to 10:30 a.m., with a laboratory session to be arranged.

Together with the description from which I quoted a moment ago, John receives a few mimeographed instructions and some words of advice from his professor. He is told that he should cover two units of laboratory work or reading per week in order to be sure of taking an A grade into his final examination; that he should withdraw from the course if he doesn't pass at least one readiness test within the first two weeks; and that a grade of Incomplete will not be given except in special cases. He is also advised that, in addition to the regular classroom hours on Tuesday and Thursday, readiness tests may be taken on Saturday mornings and Wednesday afternoons of each week—periods in which he can catch up with, or move ahead of, the rest of the class.

He then receives his first assignment: an introductory chapter from a standard textbook and two "sets" from a programmed version of similar material. With this assignment, he receives a mimeographed list of "study questions," about 30 in number. He is told to seek out the answers to these questions in his reading, so as to prepare himself for the questions he will be asked in his readiness tests. He is free to study wherever he pleases, but he is strongly encouraged to use the study hall for at least part of the time. Conditions for work are optimal there, with other students doing the same thing and with an assistant or proctor on hand to clarify a confusing passage or a difficult concept.

This is on Tuesday. On Thursday, John comes to class again, having gone through the sets of programmed material and having decided to finish his study in the classroom, where he cannot but feel that the instructor really expects him. An assistant is in charge, about half the class is there, and some late registrants are reading the course description. John tries to study his regular text, but finds it difficult to concentrate and ends by deciding to work in his room. The assistant pays no attention when he leaves.

On the following Tuesday he appears in study hall again, ready for testing, but anxious, since a whole week of the course has passed. He reports to the assistant, who sends him across the hall, without his books and notes, to the testing room, where the proctor in charge gives him a bluebook and one of the test forms for Unit 1. He takes a seat among about 20 other students and starts work. The test is composed of 10 fill-in questions and one short-answer essay question. It doesn't seem particularly difficult and, in about 10 minutes John returns his question sheet and is sent, with his bluebook, to the proctor's room for grading.

In the proctor's room, in one of 10 small cubicles, John finds his special proctor, Anne Merit. Anne is a psychology major who passed the same course earlier with a grade of A. She receives two points of credit for about 4 hours of proctoring per week, 2 hours of required attendance at a weekly proctors' meeting, and occasional extra duty in the study hall or test room. She has 9 other students besides John to look after, so she will not as a rule be able to spend much more than 5 or 10 minutes of class time with each.

Anne runs through John's answers quickly, checking two of them as incorrect and placing a question mark after his answer to the essay question. Then she asks him why he answered these three as he did. His replies show two misinterpretations of the question and one failure in written expression. A restatement of the fill-in questions and some probing with respect to the essay leads Anne to write an OK alongside each challenged answer. She congratulates John upon his performance and warns him that later units may be a little harder to master than the first.

John's success is then recorded on the wall-chart in the proctors' room, he is given his next assignment and set of study questions, and sent happily on his way. The bluebook remains with Anne, to be given later to the assistant or the instructor for inspection, and used again when John is ready for testing on Unit 2. As he leaves the room, John notices the announcement of a 20-minute lecture by his instructor, for all students who have passed Unit 3 by the following Friday, and he resolves that he will be there.

If John had failed in the defense of one or two of his answers, he would have been sent back for a minimal period of 30 minutes, for further study, with advice as to material most needing attention. If he had made more than four errors on his test, the answers would not have been considered individually; he would simply have been told that he was not ready for examination. And, if he had made no errors at all, he would probably have been asked to explain one or two of his correct answers, as a way of getting acquainted and to make sure that he was the one who had really done the work.

John did fail his first test on Unit 2, and his first two tests on Unit 4 (which gave trouble to nearly everyone). He missed the first lecture, too, but qualified for the second. (There were seven such "shows" during the term, each attended by perhaps half of the students entitled to be there.) After getting through his first five units, he failed on one review test before earning the right to move on to Unit 6. On the average, for the remainder of the course, he required nearly two readiness tests per unit. Failing a test, of course, was not an unmixed evil, since it permitted more discussion with the proctor and often served to sharpen the concepts involved.

In spite of more than a week's absence from school, John was able, by using the Wednesday and Saturday testing sessions, to complete his course units successfully about a week before the final examination. Because of his cramming for other courses during this last week, he did not review for his psychology and received only a B on his final examination. His A for the course was not affected by this, but his pride was hurt.

Sometime before the term ended, John was asked to comment on certain aspects of the course, without revealing his identity. (Remember, John is a mythical figure.) Among other things, he said that, in comparison with courses taught more conventionally, this one demanded a much greater mastery of the work assignments, it required greater memorization of detail and much greater understanding of basic concepts, it generated a greater feeling of achievement, it gave much greater recognition of the student as a person, and it was enjoyed to a much greater extent.

He mentioned also that his study habits had improved during the term, that his attitude towards testing had become more positive, that his worry about final grades had diminished, and that there had been an increase in his desire to hear lectures (this in spite of the fact that he attended only half of those for which he was qualified). When asked specifically about the use of proctors, he said that the discussions with his proctors had been very helpful, that the proctor's nonacademic, personal relation was also important to him, and that the use of proctors generally in grading and discussing tests was highly desirable.

Anne Merit, when asked to comment on her own reactions to the system, had many things to say, mostly positive. She referred especially to the satisfaction of having the respect of her proctees, of seeing them do well, and of cementing the material of the course for herself. She noted that the method was one of "mutual reinforcement" for student, proctor, assistant, and instructor. She suggested that it ought to be used in other courses and at other levels of instruction. She wondered why it would not be possible for a student to enroll in a second course immediately upon completion of the first, if it were taught by the same method. She also listed several changes that might improve the efficiency of the course machinery, especially in the area of testing and grading, where delay may sometimes occur.

In an earlier account of this teaching method (Keller, 1967b), I summarized those features which seem to distinguish it most clearly from conventional teaching procedures. They include the following:

"(1) The go-at-your-own-pace feature, *which permits a student to move through the course at a speed commensurate with his ability and other demands upon his time.*

"(2) The unit-perfection requirement for advance, *which lets the student go ahead to new material only after demonstrating mastery of that which preceded.*

"(3) The use of lectures and demonstrations as vehicles of motivation, *rather than sources of critical information.*

"(4) The related *stress upon the written word in teacher-student communication;* and, finally

"(5) The use of proctors, *which permits repeated testing, immediate scoring, almost unavoidable tutoring, and a marked enhancement of the personal-social aspect of the educational process.*"

The similarity of our learning paradigm to that provided in the field of programmed instruction is obvious. There is the same stress upon analysis of the task, the same concern with terminal performance, the same opportunity for individualized progression, and so on. But the sphere of action here is different. The principal steps of advance are not "frames" in a "set," but are more like the conventional homework assignment or laboratory exercise. "The 'response' is not simply the completion of a prepared statement through the insertion of a word or phrase. Rather, it may be thought of as the resultant of many such responses, better described as the understanding of a principle, a formula, or a concept, or the ability to use an experimental technique. Advance within the program depends on something more than the appearance of a confirming word or the presentation of a new frame; it involves a personal interaction between a student and his peer, or his better, in what may be a lively verbal interchange, of interest and importance to each participant. The use of a programmed text, a teaching machine, or some sort of computer aid within such a course is entirely possible and may be quite desirable, but it is not to be equated with the course itself." (Keller, 1967a.)

Failure to recognize that our teaching units are not as simple as the response words in a programmed text, or the letter reactions to Morse-code signals, or other comparable atoms of behavior, can lead to confusion concerning our procedure. A well-known critic of education in America, after reading an account of our method, sent me a note confessing to "a grave apprehension about the effect of breaking up the subject matter into little packages." "I should suppose," he said, "it would prevent all but the strongest minds from ever possessing a synoptic view of a field, and I imagine that the coaching, and testing, and passing in bits would amount to efficient training rather than effectual teaching."

Our "little packages" or "bits" are no smaller than the basic conceptions of a science of behavior and cannot be delivered all at once in one large synoptic parcel. As for the teaching-training distinction, one needs only to note that it is always the instructor who decides what is to be taught, and to what degree, thus determining whether he will be called a trainer or a teacher. The method he uses, the basic reinforcement contingencies he employs, may be turned to either purpose.

Many things occur, some of them rather strange, when a student is taught by a method such as ours. With respect to everyday student behavior, even a casual visit to a class will provide some novel items. For example, all the students seated in the study hall may be seen studying, undistracted by the presence or movements of others. In the test room, a student will rarely be seen chewing on his pencil, looking at a neighbor's bluebook, or staring out the window. In the crowded proctors' room, 10 pairs of students can be found concurrently engaged in academic interaction, with no couple bothered by the conversation of another, no matter how close by. Upon passing his assistant or instructor, in the corridors or elsewhere, a student will typically be seen to react in a friendly and respectful manner—enough to excite a mild alarm.

More interesting than this is the fact that a student may be tested 40 or 50 times in the course of one semester, often standing in line for the privilege, without a complaint. In one extreme instance, a student required nearly two terms to complete the work of one (after which he applied for, and got, permission to serve as a proctor for the following year).

Another unusual feature of our testing and grading is the opportunity given to defend an "incorrect" answer. This defense, as I noted earlier, may sometimes produce changes in the proctor's evaluation, changes that are regularly checked by the assistant or the instructor. Occasionally, a proctor's OK will be rejected, compelling the student to take another test, and sensitizing the proctor to the dangers of leniency; more often, it produces a note of warning, a correction, or a query written by the instructor in the student's bluebook; but always it provides the instructor with feedback on the adequacy of the question he has constructed.

Especially important, in a course taught by such a method, is the fact that any differences in social, economic, cultural, and ethnic background are completely and repeatedly subordinated to a friendly intellectual relationship between two human beings throughout a period of 15 weeks or more. Also, in such a course, a lonesome, ill-favored, underprivileged, badly schooled, or otherwise handicapped boy or girl can be assured at least a modicum of individual attention, approval, encouragement, and a chance to succeed. The only prerequisite for such treatment is a well-defined amount and quality of academic achievement.

Another oddity of the system is the production of a grade distribution that is upside down. In Figure 1 are the results from a class of 208 students at Arizona State University during the past semester. Note the diminishing relative frequency as one moves from A to D. The category of E, indicating failure, is swollen by the presence of 18 students who failed to take up their option of W (withdrawal from the course). Grades of C and D were due to the failure of students to complete all the units of reading or laboratory before going into the final examination.

Figure 1

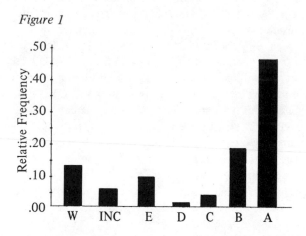

Figure 2 shows data from the class one year earlier. Essentially the same distribution holds, except for the category of Incomplete, which was then too easily obtainable. Discouraging the use of the Incomplete, together with the provision of more testing hours, apparently has the effect of regularizing study habits and equalizing the number of tests taken per week throughout the term.

116

Figure 2

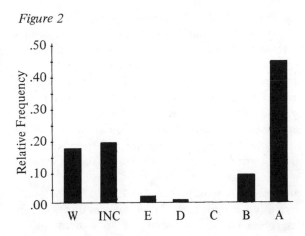

In Figure 3 (filled bars), the grade distribution is for a section of 25 students in an introductory course at Queens College (New York) during the second semester of the past school year. The same method of teaching was employed as at Arizona State, but the work requirement was somewhat greater in amount. The distinctive feature here is the relative infrequency of low grades. Only four students received less than a B rating. Professor John Farmer, who provided me with these data, reports that the two students receiving F had dropped out of the course, for unknown reasons, after seven and eight units respectively.

Figure 3

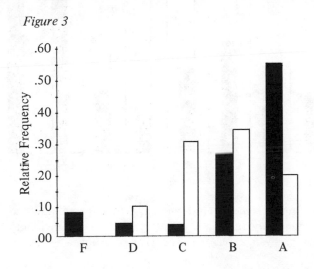

With this teaching method, students who are presumably inferior may show up better upon examination than presumably superior students taught by more conventional procedures. Figure 4 shows two distributions of grades on a midterm examination. The empty bars represent the achievement of 161 students of an Ivy League College, mainly sophomores, in the first semester of a one-year lecture-and-laboratory course in elementary psychology. The filled bars represent the achievement of 66 Arizona State University students, mainly freshmen, on an unannounced midterm quiz prepared by the Ivy League instructor and from which 13 percent of the questions had to be eliminated on the grounds of differential course coverage.

Relevant to this comparison is that pictured in Figure 3. The grade distribution obtained by Professor Farmer (and his associate, Brett Cole) is here compared with one obtained from a section of 46 students in the same course, taught in the conventional manner by a colleague who is described as "a very good instructor." The filled bars show the Farmer-Cole results; the empty ones are those from Professor Brandex.

Figure 4

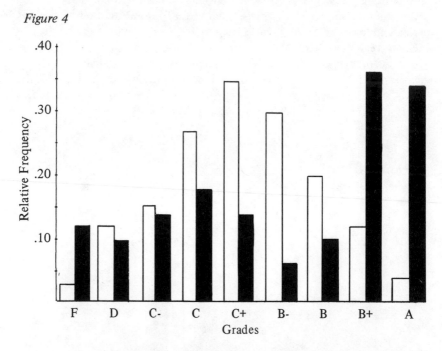

Such comparisons are of some interest and may relieve the tedium of a lecture, but they raise many questions of interpretation, and their importance should not be overemphasized. The kind of change needed in education today is not one that will be evaluated in terms of the percentage of A's in a grade distribution or of differences at the 0.01 (or 0.001) level of confidence. It is one that will produce a reinforcing state of affairs for everyone involved—a state of affairs that has heretofore been reached so rarely as to be the subject of eulogy in the world's literature, and which, unfortunately, has led to the mystique of the "great teacher" rather than a sober analysis of the critical contingencies in operation.

Our method has not yet required a grant-in-aid to keep it going. On one occasion we tried to get such help, in order to pay for mimeograph paper, the services of a clerk, and one or two additional assistants. Our request was rejected, quite properly, on the grounds that our project was "purely operational." Almost any member of a present-day fund-granting agency can recognize "research" when he sees it. I do think, however, that one should be freed, as I was, from other university demands while introducing a system like ours. And he should not be asked to teach more than two such courses regularly, each serving 100 students or less, unless he has highly qualified assistants upon whom he can depend.

Neither does the method require equipment and supplies that are not already available to almost every teacher in the country. Teaching machines, tape recorders, and computers could readily be fitted into the picture. Moving pictures and television could also be used in one or two ways without detriment to the basic educational process. But these are luxuries, based on only partial recognition of our problem, and they could divert us from more important considerations. (Proctors, like computers, may go wrong or break down, but they can often be repaired and they are easily replaced, at very little expense.)

The need for individualized instruction is widely recognized, and the most commonly suggested way of filling this need is automation. I think that this solution is incomplete, especially when applied to the young; and I'd like to mention a personal experience that bears upon the matter.

In the summer of 1966, I made numerous visits to a center for the care and treatment of autistic children.[3] One day, as I stood at the door of a classroom, I saw a boy get up from his chair at the end of a class period and give a soft pat to the object on the desk in front of him. At the same time, he said, with a slight smile, "Good-bye, Teaching Machine!"

This pseudo-social behavior in this fundamentally asocial child amused me at the time. It reminded me of Professor Moore's description of the three-year-old who became irritated when his "talking typewriter" made a mistake, called the device a "big bambam," requested its name, and ended by asking, "Who is your mother?" Today, however, I am not so sure that this is funny. It does suggest that affection may be generated within a child for an electromechanical instrument that has been essential to educational reinforcement. Unfortunately, such a machine, in its present form, is unlikely to generalize with human beings in the boy's world, giving to them a highly desirable reinforcing property. In fact, the growth of this type of student-machine relation, if it were the only one, would be a poor substitute for a directly social interaction.

In an earlier report upon our method, I mentioned that it had been anticipated, partially or *in toto,* in earlier studies, and I described one of these in some detail. As for current developments by other workers in our field, I have not made any systematic attempt to examine the offerings, even those that deal with college or university instruction. However, I have been impressed by several of them which seem to have points in common with ours, which have met with some success, and which will probably be increasingly heard from in the future.

One of these is the Audio-Tutorial Approach to the teaching of botany, developed by S. N. Postlethwait at Purdue University (Postlethwait and Novak, 1967). Another is the Socratic-Type Programming of general psychology by Harry C. Mahan (1967) and his associates at Palomar College, in California; and a third is the Interview Technique recently applied by C. B. Ferster and M. C. Perrott (1968) in teaching principles of behavior to graduate students in education at the University of Maryland.

Professor Postlethwait's method places great emphasis upon "independent study sessions" in which students carry out each individual work assignment in the course at their own pace, by means of the extensive use of tapes and films. Teaching assistants provide for oral quizzing on major concepts and help the students with difficult assignments. Weekly "small assembly sessions" are used primarily for recitation and the discussion of problems or small research projects; and "general assembly sessions" deal mainly with motivational materials. Postlethwait reports high student interest and greatly improved performance with the use of this technique. "Grades have risen from 6% A's under the conventional system to as high as 25% A's in some semesters. Failures have decreased from 20% in the conventional system to as few as 4%."

"Socratic-Type Programming" is described by Professor Mahan as "a philosophy and technology of instruction which emphasizes student response rather than presentations by the teacher. Its basic media consist of exercises made up of questions and short answers covering the content of a standard text, the text itself, tapes for recording the questions in the exercises, a classroom tape recorder for administering tests, tape duplicating facilities, a listening center in the college library, and student owned tape recorders for home use whenever possible. Classroom time is devoted largely to the discussion of points covered by the questions. All examinations are the short-answer type and are presented aurally on tape."

Students must pass three periodic tests with a score of 85% or better before they are permitted to take a comprehensive final examination. The method does not yet permit "multiple exit" from the course, but Mahan says it is "tending very much in that direction." (1967)

The Interview Technique, as described by Ferster and Perrott, does permit students to complete the course at different times, and it also approximates the student-and-proctor feature. Progress through the course is possible by verbalizing successive units of course content in a lengthy series of short interviews. The interviews are conducted mainly between students currently enrolled in the course, and any student is free to leave the course when all of his reading assignments have been adequately covered. The interviewer may sometimes be a staff member, as at the beginning of the course, but generally he is a student who has already been interviewed by someone else on the topic in question. The interviews are highly formalized, with the interviewer playing the role of the listener, checker, appraiser, and summarizer. Each interview is an open-book affair, but of such short and sharply-defined duration (10 minutes, as a rule) that the student can do no more than cue himself by reference to the printed page.

The goal of this method is nothing less than fluency with respect to each main feature of the course. Lectures, group discussions, and demonstrations are available at certain times, contingent upon a given stage of advance. Inadequate interviews are rejected, in whole or part, without prejudice, and with suggestions for further study. A product of high quality is guaranteed through staff participation at critical points. A modification of this procedure, which is to include written tests and the employment of advanced-student proctors, is planned by Professor Ferster for the introductory course in psychology at Georgetown University during the coming semester.

In systems like these, and in the one I have centered on, the work of a teacher is at variance with that which has predominated in our time. His public appearances as classroom entertainer, expositor, critic, and debater no longer seem important. His principal job, as Frank Finger (1962) once defined it, is truly "the facilitation of learning in others." He becomes an educational engineer, a contingency manager, with the responsibility of serving the great majority, rather than the small minority, of young men and women who come to him for schooling in the area of his competence. The teacher of tomorrow will not, I think, continue to be satisfied with a 10% efficiency (at best) which makes him an object of contempt by some, commiseration by others, indifference by many, and love by a few. No longer will he need to hold his position by the exercise of functions that neither transmit culture, dignify his status, nor encourage respect for learning in others. No longer will he need to live, like Ichabod Crane, in a world that increasingly begrudges him room and lodging for a doubtful service to its young. A new kind of teacher is in the making. To the old kind I, for one, will be glad to say "Good-bye!"

I started this paper on a personal note and I would like to end it on one. Twenty-odd years ago, when white rats were first used as laboratory subjects in the introductory course, a student would sometimes complain about his animal's behavior. The beast couldn't learn, he was asleep, he wasn't hungry, he was sick, and so forth. With a little time and a handful of pellets, we could usually show that this was wrong. All that one needed to do was follow the rules. "The rat," we used to say, "is always right."

My days of teaching are over. After what I have said about efficiency, I cannot lay claim to any great success, but my schedule of rewards was enough to maintain my behavior, and I learned one very important thing: *the student is always right.* He is not asleep, not unmotivated, not sick, and he can learn a great deal if we provide the right contingencies of reinforcement. But if we don't provide them, and provide them soon, he too may be inspired to say "Good-bye!" to formal education.

Notes

1. With the aid of (Dr.) Lanny Fields and the members of a senior seminar at Columbia College, during the fall term of 1963-64.

2. For example, by J. L. Michael with high school juniors on a National Science Foundation project at Grinnell College (Iowa), in 1965; and by J. Farmer and B. Cole at Queens College (New York) in a course similar to the one described here.

3. At the Linwood Children's Center, Ellicott City, Maryland.

References

Ferster, C. B. & Perrott, M. C. *Behavior Principles.* New York: Appleton-Century-Crofts, 1968.

Finger, F. W. Psychologists in colleges and universities. In W. B. Webb (Ed.), *The Profession of Psychology.* New York: Holt, Reinhart and Winston, 1962.

Keller, F. S. Studies in international Morse code: I. A new method of teaching code reception. *Journal of Applied Psychology,* 1943, *27,* 407-415.

Keller, F. S. A personal course in psychology. In R. Ulrich, T. Stachnik, and J. Mabry (Eds.), *The Control of Behavior.* Glenview, Ill.: Scott, Foresman, 1966.

Keller, F. S. Engineering personalized instruction in the classroom. *Revista Interamericana de Psicologia,* 1967a, *1,* 189-197.

Keller, F. S. Neglected rewards in the educational process. *Proceedings of the 23rd American Conference of Academic Deans,* Los Angeles, CA, January 1967b.

Keller, F. S. & Schoenfeld, W. N. The psychology curriculum at Columbia College. *American Psychologist,* 1949, *4,* 165-172.

Mahan, H. C. The use of Socratic type programmed instruction in college courses in psychology. Paper read at Western Psychological Association, San Francisco, May, 1967.

Postlethwait, S. N. & Novak, J. D. The use of 8mm loop films in individualized instruction. *Annals of the New York Academy of Science,* 1967, Vol. 142, Art. 2, 464-470.

Sherman, J. G. Application of reinforcement principles to a college course. Paper read at American Educational Resources Association, New York, February 1967.

10

"English Spoken Here"

A continuing result of my experience in Brazil and with Brazilians has been my interest in the Portuguese language. One of the most satisfying events of my life, perhaps, was on July 5th, 1972, when I delivered an address to the Brazilian Society for the Progress of Science, at the University of Sao Paulo—an address that was composed and delivered in the *lingua da terra*. The following note is another outcome of my South American exposure.

This paper is reprinted from the *Psychological Record*, 1970, *20*, 262-269. It is reprinted with permission from the *Psychological Record*.

I have been looking again at Boring's 1956 comments on the place of foreign-language study in the training of psychologists in the United States (Boring, 1956). The isolationism which he describes as protruding thousands of miles from our shores is even greater today than it was 14 years ago, and it seems to be growing worse. Our countless economic pressures on other nations of the world, our far-flung military camps and colonies, and our new devices for bringing the American voice into every nook and cranny of the earth's surface (and beyond)—these and other factors, some of them purely local, seem to be lessening our desire to master any other tongue but English.

Professor Boring made two points: (a) foreign-language mastery serves international comprehension (which is good) and should not be tossed aside without a replacement that will do the job as well; and (b) language learning, like basic research, should be maintained because of long-run scientific dividends, rather than immediate practical gains. Unfortunately, neither point has much appeal for the curriculum maker of today. He knows, probably from his own experience, the depths to which the word *mastery* has fallen; and he is reluctant to argue 'future values' to students who are demanding relevance *now*.

He may see the sense in teaching Thai to military men and State Department workers, or Spanish to agents of Standard Oil or General Motors, although he may not approve of the ultimate goals; but how can he honestly recommend the protracted study of French, German, or Russian (pick two) to his young colleagues-to-be when he recalls how *he* was taught, what he actually learned, and how much use he has made of it since? Better, by far, that they have more mathematics; and let them buy, when and if the time comes, whatever translations they may need.

My sympathies are with Boring. I believe that "a community of scholarship is good for civilization"; and that a language requirement may serve such a community. But I can also hear the opposition's plaint and feel its force. The kind of requirement that Boring sponsored, and his pupils tried to meet, was a failure. Let me be a witness to this fact.

I passed my own French examinations after three college courses in the subject (in which I did badly), two visits to France, and the translation of Buytendijk's *Psychologie des Animaux,* Pieron's *Psychologie Experimentale,* Kellogg's *L'Enfant et le Singe,* and a few other items. I met the German requirement, on the second try (or the third), after a trip to Germany, a summer course at Harvard (*Immensee* and *Karl Heinrich*), a month in Vienna, a translation of H. E. Ziegler's *Tierpsychologie* and about two-thirds of Mach's *Bewegungsempfindungen,* along with papers by Narziss Ach and one or two others. I have used both languages since then, especially the French, but I can't read German today without a dictionary,

I speak neither French nor German well enough to carry on an intelligent discussion, my writing is hopeless, and I get very little satisfaction from whatever skill I may retain.

If this were my only experience, I would find it hard to support a foreign-language requirement in any graduate program; but I have other testimony to present. In 1961, I taught for a year at the University of Sao Paulo. Before I left this country, I took a summer course in Portuguese and, during my stay in Brazil, I sought to learn as much of the language as I could, in spite of English-speaking pupils, colleagues, and friends. Upon my return to the States, I continued my study, mainly by reading a few Brazilian novels. In 1964, I spent another term in the country, lecturing in (bad) Portuguese, and improving my writing and hearing skills as much as circumstances permitted. Since then I have maintained my interest in the language with a few minutes of daily reading, a little tutorial aid, and an occasional Brazilian visitor.

I still stumble in my speaking, am somewhat slow in hearing, and have trouble with the subjunctive. I despair of ever being truly bilingual. But I now have two countries in which I feel at home, two cultures to enjoy, two scientific bodies of which I am a part, two educational systems to compare, two (or more) political philosophies to assess, and, in effect, two worlds in which I freely move, where I used to have but one.

What can one conclude, from such experiences as these, about the wisdom of foreign-language training for our psychologists of tomorrow? Nothing at all, perhaps, but I'd still like to have my say about the matter.

1. A "reading knowledge" of any foreign language is a joke. It may have some slight value as a preliminary step towards scholarly interaction, but no more. It is limited in reach, inefficient in use, and hard to maintain. As a device for international communication, it is almost worthless, and the sooner it is ditched the better.
2. A *working* knowledge of a language is another story. If one can read, speak, and write a second tongue, and understand its spoken form, his sphere of useful action as a scientist and scholar may be greatly enhanced and his personal life may be greatly enriched.
3. If I could have my way, I would ask each first-year graduate student in my field to select a second *country* and perfect himself as far as possible in its geography, history, development of psychology, and especially its language. He might study French, German, Spanish, Russian, or the idiom of any land wherein existed a psychological community of appreciable size. (I imagine he would pick a language he had already begun, but this I would not require; I would ask only that it be available for study. And I wouldn't call on him for anything new if his

family origins already gave him a second-language skill.)

I would then enroll the candidate in a course on *International Psychology,* or something of the sort, for which credit would be given upon the completion of certain prescribed tasks and the demonstration of a *functional* language proficiency, however crude, in conversing, corresponding, and lecturing, as well as the translation of an article or so for the departmental library.

In this course, I would expect him to report informally on the current status of some psychological specialization within the country he has chosen; on the general system of education that prevails therein; and, perhaps, on the customs and cultural achievements of its people. I might also expect him to act as a cicerone for any visitors to the department from 'his country'; to help the Admissions Committee evaluate the academic qualifications of any students from there who apply for graduate status; and to assist in building a descriptive file of the country's outstanding psychologists.

I would also encourage him to prepare, if circumstances permitted, for a post-doctoral period of study within his chosen domain, or even a *Wanderjahr.* I'd advise him that 'Fulbrights' sometimes go to the man who knows the host country's language, even when his other credentials are extremely weak; and I'd acquaint him with the fact that we are seldom represented in international councils by our best-regarded colleagues, for reasons much the same. I would describe the scholarly interaction that is possible, and sometimes carried out, between two countries—e.g., between Brazilian and American centers in physiology, chemistry, anthropology, and genetics. Students and professors go back and forth between such centers, with profit and with pleasure. And, finally, I would tell him how he might at least spend an interesting sabbatical year, if earlier contacts with his country could not be conveniently arranged.

The learning task is not as great as I may have implied. Just one foreign language is involved, and most students already have a little background when they embark on graduate study. A few might have no need at all for further training. For those who may be weak, there are refresher courses and programmed offerings in growing number with which to remedy one's deficiencies. A kind of "language lab" within one's own department would not, perhaps, be out of the question. Also, within the motivating context I've suggested, progress would be more rewarding and learning more fun than it has been in the past.

The effects of such a requirement, if widely adopted, would soon be felt at the undergraduate level, where majors in our field would find reason to acquire the facility they need in advance of graduate study. Language teachers would, I am sure, be grateful for the interest we engendered, and might come to view us as collaborators in the attainment of their goals.

The program outlined here is far from perfect, but it is meaningful, and it could be set up and rigorously administered with less work, less pain, less intellectual dishonesty, and far more profit than those that currently prevail. It might have been better, as Professor Boring argued, if Latin had never been replaced in the discourse of scientists and scholars. A single extra language would then have served for all—might even have become the vulgate. But this seems out of the question now, and no suggested substitute has yet found wide acceptance.

Meanwhile, as the rest of the world gets closer, we are moving further away from it. Less and less do we talk, as scientists or simply as human beings, with our counterparts in other lands. Our principal agents of international understanding are the businessman, the soldier, and the tourist who looks into every shop window for *English Spoken Here*. To bring a realistic language requirement into our graduate psychology programs would not greatly alter the balance of understanding between men and nations in our time, but it would be a step in the right direction.

References

Boring, E. G. Isolationism in the language requirement. *Contemporary Psychology,* 1956, *1,* 331-332.

11

An International Venture in Behavior Modification

In February of 1971 I was invited by Emilio Ribes Inesta to be the honorary chairman of the 2nd Symposium on Behavior Modification, which was to be held at the University of Vera Cruz the following January. (The site was later changed to the Federal University in Mexico City.) I took this as an opportunity to describe the beginnings of PSI (personalized system of instruction) and to bring up to date my thoughts upon the matter.

There is a practice among the people of my country called *retirement*. It is carried out by workers in many organizations and many institutions. At Columbia University, for example, a professor must stop teaching when he reaches the age of 65 or, at the latest, 68. If he should be an officer of administration, whose duties require greater powers of the mind, he *must* retire at 65, although he may go on *to teach* for three years more. These rules are based upon the wisdom of our leaders, who know exactly when the little grey cells within the brain begin to suffer a collapse.

With these hard facts of life and physiology to guide me, I began to think about my own retirement well before the time when it was scheduled to occur. I commenced to look around for a warmer, less expensive climate than that of New York City. I thought of Puerto Rico and Southern California; for awhile I even thought of Cuba, but the climate there became almost *too* warm.

Then, quite suddenly, I received an invitation to Brazil. It came from Myrthes Rodrigues do Prado, a student at the University of Sao Paulo. Myrthes had been a pupil of mine at Columbia several years before, but had been compelled to leave her course because of a serious illness. She wrote me to ask if I would consider coming to Sao Paulo as a visiting professor.

I was sure that Myrthes, only a student, had little right to be extending invitations to professors, but I was flattered by her letter nevertheless. I wrote a pleasant answer, expressing interest in South America and a desire for further information. Then I dropped the matter, except for looking at a map to find out where Brazil would be, and speaking briefly with my colleague, Otto Klineberg, who had once been there.

That was in May of 1959. In December I received another letter from my former pupil and, a few days later, a cablegram from Dr. Paulo Sawaya, the well-known physiologist, who was then Director of the Faculty of Philosophy, Sciences, and Letters at the University of Sao Paulo. He offered me a chair in experimental psychology. I decided that Myrthes, although just a little girl, must have a lot of power.

I replied to Dr. Sawaya's cable with another, again expressing interest, but requesting further information. He answered me with a letter which didn't explain very much, but told me how happy he was to know that I would come. He suggested also that, in addition to my teaching, there were pressing psychological problems that I could easily solve within the University when I got there. If I had been a little less romantic or a little more perceptive, I might have read between the lines and stayed at home.

Many things took place within the year that followed. My manager, and center of my affection, had to be convinced that I was not insane; our house had to be rented; a leave of absence had to be arranged; and a loss of income had to be looked after by a Fulbright-Hayes award. We underwent innoculations and bought all-purpose clothing that could be washed in any jungle stream. I took a summer course in Portuguese at Columbia with three other students, taught by an engineer from Lisboa. Except for the Berlitz School, I could find no other place in New York City in which one could prepare to speak with 80 million "good neighbors" in Brazil. (I later learned that this one did not prepare me either.)

Finally, I was talked to by the State Department concerning "culture shock" and related matters, with examples drawn from Indonesian sources, except for one or two from Chile and Peru. Then, on a cold February evening in 1961, we took off from Idlewild Airport on the overnight flight to Rio, loaded down with erroneous ideas and 40 kilos of excess baggage. Five days later, after an official "orientation" (mostly on the beach of Copacabana), we arrived in Sao Paulo.

We were met by Dr. Sawaya, who had just been relieved of his duties as Director of the Faculty. He was accompanied by his successor, Dr. Mario Guimaraes Ferri, and by Dr. Carolina Martuscelli Bori. Dona Carolina went with us that night to dinner and tried, without success, to clarify the local academic and political situation. It was obvious that I had a lot to learn within the year ahead.

Among the things that happened soon was a memorable encounter with Dr. Anita Cabral and a group of her assistants and co-workers in psychology at the University. It had not been *her* idea that I should come to Sao Paulo. In fact, she had a different plan entirely, but this I did not know. As soon as the formalities were over and we were seated at her conference table, she went directly to the point: "I hope," she said, "that you bring us something new—something that we do not already know."

Dona Anita was really not expressing a hope, nor was she being very kind to her embarrassed guest, but she was asking a very important question—a question that should be put to every teacher before he accepts an invitation to be a visiting professor in a foreign land: Is there a plausible academic reason for this journey? There are, perhaps, no better emissaries from one nation to another than its students and professors; but there must be something for the student to gain from his study that he could not get at home, and there must be something new, in terms of knowledge or of skill, that the professor carries with him if his appointment is to be worthwhile.

What I took to Brazil in 1961 were the seeds of reinforcement theory, and they fell on very fertile soil. My third- and fourth-year pupils at the University of Sao Paulo, both men and women, were especially alert to new ideas. Their number wasn't very large (10 or 15 at the most), but the quality of their understanding was as great as any teacher could desire.

In addition to the "experimental analysis of behavior," I brought a piece of apparatus to Brazil (at least it started out for there when I did) and a special kind of textbook in which many critical words were missing from each page but could be found upon the next one. The Skinner Box permitted us to carry on research in animal learning before the year had ended; and the Holland-Skinner programmed text was translated into Portuguese by Rodolpho Azzi and is still in use today.

Rodolpho was my first *assistente* and he made the difference between success and failure in my work at Sao Paulo. His advice and counsel saved me from humiliation or disaster on more than one occasion. His experience in teaching and his keen awareness of my problems often helped to bridge the gap of understanding between me and my pupils. His patience and good humor were often put to test but never failed.

Besides Rodolpho, there was Dr. Martuscelli Bori, the psychologist who had greeted us upon arriving in Sao Paulo. Dona Carolina, in spite of her many other duties, found the time to attend my classes, to do the laboratory work connected with them, and to participate in several research efforts. Her support was critical in furthering the growth of reinforcement theory in Brazil and, with Rodolpho Azzi, she later took an active part in the educational venture that I am going to describe.

By the time that I was ready to go home, some progress had been made. In spite of interruptions produced by student strikes, the abdication of Janio Quadros, and other events of lesser importance, a number of items could be listed. Our course had been successfully completed by almost all of our students; two collaborative studies had been prepared for publication;[1] a primitive laboratory had been constructed for experiments in animal behavior; three students had applied for foreign study and were soon to be accepted; and I had succeeded in persuading John Gilmour Sherman, a former pupil and co-worker at Columbia, to come to Sao Paulo in 1962.

It would have been hard to find a better man than Gilmour Sherman for building up a laboratory and consolidating theory at the University of Sao Paulo. "Gil," as everyone called him, was effective from the start, and readily adjusted to the Brazilian *ambiente*. (On his first evening in Sao Paulo, he was made to feel almost as much at home as in New York; two *ladroes*,* whom he met on the street, relieved him of all his ready money.) His classes were popular, his laboratory prospered, he worked well with all his colleagues, and his progress in speaking Portuguese was exceptionally good.

*Thieves

Near the end of his year at Sao Paulo, Sherman went with Dr. Martuscelli Bori and Rodolpho Azzi to Brasilia. They were invited by Darcy Ribeiro, *Chefe do Gabinete Civil* under Joao Goulart, who was then recruiting teachers for the national university. Darcy was a former colleague at Sao Paulo, and wanted Dona Carolina to come to Brasilia, with a staff of her own selection, to build a Department of Psychology in the new University. Darcy charmed the members of the group and excited them with the prospect of creating a splendid department, along whatever lines they chose to follow with respect to orientation, curriculum, and procedures of instruction. They were so enthusiastic and persuasive in the letters which they wrote to me that I agreed to join them. (I did not tell them that the time was approaching when my little grey cells would diminish in their function.)

As a first step in our project, my friends came to the United States. There they visited universities, hospitals, and other centers where psychology was taught, studied, or practiced in one way or another. They talked with teachers, researchers, and clinicians. They went to laboratories, libraries, and machine shops. They took notes on everything and tried to extract from every experience something of value to our program.

They bought or were given hundreds of books, and they ordered laboratory apparatus. They got many words of advice and counsel from psychologists who were later to become a corps of departmental consultants. And, finally, at the end of their travels, we all sat down around the fire in Englewood, New Jersey, at my home, to discuss our next objectives.

We began with the curriculum problem at Brasilia and were soon involved in a consideration of the introductory course of study. The University was to open soon and we would have to be ready for those students of the first year who had picked psychology as their chosen field of science. While we were teaching them their ABC's, we could prepare the courses that would follow.

We quickly agreed upon the content of this course, but not upon the way it should be taught. The more we considered our customary methods and the criticisms of them which my visitors had collected, the more unsuitable they seemed for South American export. We began to worry about matters that hadn't bothered us before, or matters that we had felt we could not change. We talked about the pros and cons of the lecture system; the validity of examinations; the significance of letter or number grades; the rigid frame of hours, months, or years into which our course materials were supposed to fit; and so on. And we continually tried to relate these matters to current applications of the analysis of behavior.

Darcy Ribeiro had encouraged my colleagues to be experimental, with respect to form as well as content of our teaching. Here was a chance to break away from old procedures. What about programmed instruction, for example? All of us knew about teaching machines and programmed textbooks. Rodolpho's translation of *Holland and Skinner* has been mentioned; Gil Sherman had bought a teaching machine while at Barnard College and had written a program for it; and I had conducted a Columbia College seminar on this technique of instruction.

My friends had also been impressed by what they had heard and seen in Professor Skinner's Natural Science course at Harvard, and by the Behavioral Technology course that Charles Ferster had begun at the Institute for Behavioral Research in Maryland. Charles had prepared a sequence of experiments for the individual instruction of new staff members and visitors at the Institute. He would first expose his pupils to a fairly complicated study, letting each of them control the behavior of a pigeon by simply turning on and off a light within the bird's experimental chamber. After that, each student had to work his way alone through all the stages needed to achieve the same result as that which he had initially witnessed.

The result of our discussion was a plan which I described in my diary that night as a combination of Columbia, Harvard, and I.B.R. procedures which promised to become [I quote] "one of the most exciting and most radical ever given in a university setting."[2] One month later (April 29th), I was more explicit. "The Education program. . . represents a distillation of many things: the method of laboratory teaching at Columbia—in Psychology 1-2 and Psychology 127 [a sequence of experiments for individual graduate students] ; the method used at I.B.R.; the use of programmed instruction where possible; the treatment of textbooks, lectures, conferences, etc., as *rewards* for passing through various stages of individual study and experimentation; the use of lectures as inspirational rather than truly instructional; the measurement of progress by compilation of things the student has successfully done, rather than by grades on examinations."

Soon after we made our tentative decision, my friends went back to Sao Paulo, to fill in details of our plan and otherwise prepare for the new Department. I agreed to join them when my obligations at Columbia were discharged. Then I went back to conventional teaching for one more term. I found it very difficult, however, to think about anything but Brasilia and our future operations there.

By August of 1965 my commitment to the project was so great that I went on record at the Philadelphia meetings of the American Psychological Association with the description of a course that had never yet been given . . . [*A Personal Course in Psychology,* see page 99] .

Today, nine years after this report was written, I am amazed at the similarity of this imaginary course to the one that was actually taught in

Brasilia, and the really small number of basic changes in the format that have since been made. The daily *modus operandi* was altered slightly, the emphasis on laboratory work decreased, the *student proctor* was added to our staff, and we didn't get rid of letter grades entirely. But the self-pacing feature, the performance requirement for advance, the downgrading of the lecture, and the general spirit of the course remains the same.

In my final term at Columbia, I sent up a trial balloon. With the aid of my graduate assistant, Lanny Fields, and five seniors in the College, I constructed a miniature program along the lines I've just described. Then, in the Christmas recess of 1963, this course was offered to three students—two high-school seniors and a college freshman—who agreed to act as subjects. Based on five experiments, the course was programmed in every detail, including equipment, procedures, and reading assignments. I talked to the class but once, on the first day of the course, and my assistant's interactions with the students were limited almost entirely to testing and handing out assignments. More than any other course I've taught, this one ran itself. And I would never give a course like it again!

My three young guinea-pigs were positive, however, in their reactions to the course. They worked efficiently on their own, progressing at slightly different rates, and all of them were "graduated" within the vacation period. Their only complaint, which was not very loud and which I was too busy to hear, concerned the lack of opportunity for discussion. They wanted, and should have had, someone with whom to talk about their work.

One month later, on a Liberty Ship from World War I, bearing the Liberian flag, manned by Greeks, and carrying phosphate from Florida to Brazil, my wife and I set out on a 22-day voyage to join our colleagues for the next stage of our venture. She had definitely decided I was crazy, but didn't feel she should desert me at a time when I needed her so much.

Our group had been working hard in Sao Paulo, assembling equipment, collecting books, and discussing our basic plan. They were making final preparations for the move to Brasilia, where the space for our Department had been allocated and could soon be occupied. Then, suddenly, the nation underwent a governmental change. Joao Goulart was out of office and the country, and so was Darcy Ribeiro. The University was closed and we were left without a home for our Department. It appeared that our beautiful dream was shattered.

The Americans in our group prepared to leave the country since they no longer held appointments and there was nothing else to do. We advanced the date of our employment at Arizona State University, where we were promised freedom to engage in teaching innovations. We still met together often, as if we had a future, but our meetings lacked purpose and enthusiasm. We felt that we were simply killing time.

It takes weeks, however, to leave Brazil, in any kind of political weather; and, before the date of our departure, Dr. Zeferino Vaz, the new Rector at the University of Brasilia, asked us to continue with our program. After some confusion, we agreed to do so. Early in May of 1964 our little group of *bandierantes** advanced upon the capital city, ready to set up in business once again.

Nevertheless, our project had been delayed in its inauguration, and Sherman and I were far away in Arizona when the course which we had helped to conceive finally got started. It was in early August when Rodolpho Azzi, with the support of his coordinator and a dedicated staff of young assistants, brought *personalized instruction* to the University of Brasilia.

This course has never been described in detail, and I cannot do so here, but something must be said about it. It was a systematic course, an introduction to reinforcement theory. Each student progressed within it *at his own pace,* through 42 units of work, including 12 experiments that came early in the course. In contrast with the current format, in the United States and elsewhere, there were no letter grades, no occasional lectures or discussions, no final examinations, and no student proctors. The experiments were evaluated by several assistants, most of them above the fourth-year level, and "reading checks" or unit tests were looked after by a Departmental clerk, known to all as Senhor Daniel.

In our original plan, the course was to have three parts, each of which, in deference to tradition, was to require about one term for its completion. Only the first two parts were actually taught, however, before a University convulsion brought our whole curriculum, and many others, to its end. Part I was twice presented in this period, with excellent results from both a student and a faculty point of view. All but one or two of the 50 students in the first term completed their work successfully within the time allotted—a fact that may be due to the many opportunities that they had for testing and retesting.

When asked about the course's most agreeable feature, the students usually said *self-pacing,* going at one's own speed—a "more responsible" way of working, as one of them described it. The *least* agreeable feature of the course appeared to be its failure to provide for discussion of the reading assignments with someone better qualified than Senhor Daniel.

Except for Rodolpho Azzi, who turned to another sphere of applied behavior analysis, the members of the Brasilia staff moved on to other teaching positions in other institutions. What would have happened if they

*Flag bearers

could have stayed together and the program had been continued we shall never know. Our original aim had been to let one course of study lead naturally into another, without delay, in accordance with the student's readiness and desire, until his training was complete. If this had been permitted to occur, these students might have been the first to show the way, by their example, of liberating higher education from the calendar and the clock. Instead, we had to take a slower, northern route, by way of Arizona, and we are only now arriving at this destination.

In the spring of 1965, at Arizona State University, two variations of the Brasilia Plan were used in teaching introductory courses in the principles of behavior. In one of these, my own, ten student aides, called *proctors,* took the place of Senhor Daniel in grading unit tests, for a class of 94 students. In the other, taught by Gilmour Sherman and involving fewer students, this function was performed by the instructor, with the help of a graduate assistant. Both courses were sufficiently successful to encourage further exploration.

Within a few semesters we had reached a basic pattern of procedure— one that I have since described many times and in many places.[3] In all but one respect it was simply a refinement and extension of the Brasilia plan, modified to meet the grim realities of the scene in an educationally under-developed country. At the risk of becoming an irritating echo, I shall enumerate once more the fundamental features of our system.

In the first place, as I noted before, the student is permitted to advance within a course of study at the rate which he himself prefers, within broad limits.

Secondly, there is a specified and high degree of mastery demanded in connection with each unit—something that can only be assured with student pacing.

Thirdly, the system permits repeated testing, with no loss of credit or of status in the case of failure, and with ample opportunity for the student to defend his answers.

Fourthly, in order to provide for this testing and individual evaluation, the system typically makes use of *proctors*—well-instructed and carefully directed students who have demonstrated that they understand the material in question.

Finally, the plan avoids, as far as possible, group instruction, or any other method in which there is no *quid pro quo*. This includes the usual lecture, the usual demonstration or other "visual aid," the usual discussion group, and the usual assignment of a paper to be written. Any so-called learning situation in which the objectives are unspecified, the behavior may be absent, or the rewards are noncontingent, is not a learning situation worthy of the name, even if it should be one in which some learning

140

can occur.

In these features of the Arizona version of our Brasilia plan, the student of behavior modification will discover most of the conditions of effective learning. He will recognize that we tried to guarantee for student, proctor, and professor a high frequency of generalized reinforcement, of every kind within our reach, and a minimal degree of punishment and opportunity for extinction. In addition, we attempted to create an interlocking system, with each participant deriving his duties, as well as his rewards, from the activities of the others. We wanted a system of mutual reinforcement, mutual dependence, and mutual tuition.

As soon as it was clear that students, proctors, and graduate assistants liked what we were doing, and that the University administration did not view us as subversives, I began to write and lecture on our plan, suggesting that we had the answer to democratic education. Gilmour Sherman was too young to take such chances, and too busy with other academic obligations, so I became the spokesman for the group, at least in the United States.

The reaction of other teachers was, at first, depressing. I found that most of my colleagues were indifferent, condescending, or openly hostile. They applauded our efforts, on occasion, then instantly analyzed the method and decided it was not for them, for reasons that did not always seem profound. This was especially true of my closest colleagues, and still is (which may suggest a special knowledge that the others don't possess).

There were, however, a few exceptions—relatives, friends, or former pupils who thought the scheme worth trying and found, to their great satisfaction, that I had not lied about it. These teachers sometimes led others to adopt the same procedure, and they became the spearhead of a movement which now disturbs me in its magnitude and in the liberties taken with the basic format.

Examples of our plan in use now range throughout the academic spectrum and beyond. I have heard of courses in anthropology, astronomy, and art; in biology, business, and biophysics; in chemistry, electronics, education, and engineering (chemical, civil, electrical, mechanical, and nuclear); in geology, history, language, mathematics, medicine, music, and nurses' training; in physics, physiology, religion, sociology, and statistics, in addition to psychology, where it all began.

There are university departments in which the plan is used in every course; there is at least one college in which a student may earn his bachelor's degree without departing from our format; and I know of several applications outside the academic sphere. I have also heard of masters' essays and a doctoral dissertation devoted to the history and current status of our venture. I expect at any time to hear that we have been denounced by some teachers college or some school of education—the ultimate sign of our success.

As a specific instance of what is going on, let me mention a meeting last November which Dr. Sherman and I attended. It was a two-day conference on our plan, at the Massachusetts Institute of Technology, arranged by its Education Research Center. The meeting was conducted by Dr. Ben A. Green, a physicist at the Center, and was attended by about 300 teachers, from all over the United States and several foreign lands. They represented many fields of science and the humanities, especially the former. Most of them were not psychologists, but nearly all of them were teaching with our Brasilia-Arizona method, or getting ready to do so.

Several features of this conference impressed me greatly. In spite of widely different backgrounds and long histories of insulation from each other, these teachers got along extremely well together. They displayed a common purpose—to improve their teaching; they had similar findings to report and experiences to be shared; and they showed an enthusiasm for our system that was (if you will pardon an expression) highly reinforcing to Sherman and to me. We felt like soldiers in a great crusade, and we wished that our Brazilian comrades could have been there.

Whether this particular system will survive is, of course, a question that I cannot answer here. But I feel safe in making one or two predictions. I believe the world is going to see an enormous change in its techniques of education within the coming years. This change will not result primarily from automation, televised instruction, information theory, sensitivity training, miracle drugs, or student participation in curricular decision making, whatever the value of any of these may be. Nor will it necessarily follow great expenditures of money.

It will come, instead, from "behavior analysis applied to education," as this symposium suggests, of which the Brasilia Plan is only one example. It will eventually maximize the pleasure of scholarly endeavor and occupational training, for the old as well as for the young. In our educational institutions, it will involve less emphasis on rigid time requirements and more on quality of achievement; greater opportunity for success, but with nothing provided *gratis;* with more privacy for the person and less invidious comparison with others; and a greater respect for human dignity than has ever been shown before in formal education.

I can also imagine a day when the length of any course of study will depend entirely upon its content and the student who undertakes it; when letter or number grades have disappeared or have been vested with new meaning; when no student is advanced in status unless he has deserved it; when everyone is free to "drop out" and return to study when he chooses; and when the use of well-controlled and well-instructed *proctors* will be a common feature in the practice of medicine, law, and other highly skilled vocations. But now my crystal ball grows cloudy.

I have tried to tell you the story of a venture in behavior modification—of the origins, the growth, and the final form of a system of instruction. I have sought to give you an idea of this system's present status, and I have guessed about the future. There is only one more comment to be made.

I have stressed the international aspect of our venture, mainly because it was developed in the United States and in Brazil, by citizens of each country. It did not involve, however, any summit meetings between John F. Kennedy and Janio Quadros; Lyndon Johnson didn't visit Joao Goulart to talk about it; and I am certain that Richard Nixon never brought the matter up with Humberto Castelo Branco or in his recent conversation with President Medici. There has been no complicated interchange of diplomatic missions. No *hot line* was established for quick communication on the subject of our plan. There was just an unpretentious and cooperative interaction of four teachers, trained in the analysis of behavior, and dedicated to the proposition that something useful might be done about the educational problem. That may have been sufficient.

Notes

1. (a) Azzi, R., Fix, D. S. R., Rocha e Silva & Keller, F. S. Exteroceptive control of response under delayed reinforcement. *Journal of Experimental Analysis of Behavior,* 1964, 7, 159-162.

(b) Azzi, R., Rocha e Silva, M. I., Bori, C. M., Fix, D. S. R., & Keller, F. S. Suggested Portuguese translation of expressions in operant conditioning. *Journal of Experimental Analysis of Behavior,* 1963, 6, 91-94.

2. Keller, F. S. A personal course in psychology. In R. Ulrich, T. Stachnik and J. Mabry (Eds.), *The Control of Behavior.* Glenview, IL.: Scott, Foresman, 1966.

3. Keller, F. S. "Good-bye, teacher . . ." *Journal of Applied Behavior Analysis,* 1968, *1,* 78-89. (This is the best known of the papers dealing with the Brasilia Plan in the United States.) See page 105, this volume.

12

Ten Years of
Personalized Instruction

In the summer of 1974, I was asked to write a paper on the first ten years of a *personalized system of instruction,* PSI, for readers of a new journal, *Teaching of Psychology.* The request was made by J. Russell Nazzaro, Administrative Officer of Educational Affairs, of the American Psychological Association, in behalf of Robert S. Daniel, the editor of the journal. "Russ" was one of my former pupils at Columbia, an old friend, and an early user of the Brasilia plan in the United States. He and his wife, Jean, had followed Sherman and me at the University of Brasilia, and were teaching there at the time when Rodolfo Azzi and co-workers formally launched the system in their first-year course in the analysis of behavior.

After weighing pros and cons, I decided to accept the invitation. Although excellent reviews of PSI (by James Kulik and associates, by Donald Cook, and by Robert Ruskin) had already been written, none was aimed precisely at the audience in question—the working teacher of our science. I saw an opportunity to bring psychologists up to date, and to tell them how the plan was faring elsewhere; to make another plea to the would-be user that he follow our prescription once, at least, *before* he introduced his changes for the better; and, finally, to bring things into focus for myself as I carried out the task.

The result was the present offering, here reproduced with permission of *Teaching of Psychology.* The first and the third of my goals—the summary and the perspective—may have been attained to some extent, but I have my doubts about the second. Any attempt to get one student of the learning-teaching process to follow the directions of another is probably doomed to failure from the start!

This paper is reprinted from the *Teaching of Psychology*, 1974, *1*, 4-9. It is reprinted with permission from *Teaching of Psychology*.

Some years ago, perhaps in 1966, the Editor of the *Newsletter* for Division 2 of the American Psychological Association sent out a call for new ideas on the teaching of psychology. I responded with a brief account of a system of instruction that J. G. Sherman and I were using in an elementary course at Arizona State University. Then I watched successive issues of the *Newsletter* to see if my contribution would be printed.

In the months that followed, I read about some interesting innovations in the field, including one in which the teacher sat in the back of the room and let his pupils run the class, but my own donation was never among them. Finally, in compliance with a well-known law of behavior, I stopped looking. But I was still of the opinion that the method we were using was a good one, and I continued to promote it when and where I could. I talked about it to psychologists at nearby institutions and, on one occasion, I made a speech about it at the American Conference of Academic Deans,[1] with very little impact as far as I could tell, though my enthusiasm was applauded.

A second chance to reach Division 2 appeared in 1967 when its President (Neil Bartlett) asked me to tell my story to the membership, at the Washington meetings of the A.P.A. My feelings of rejection dissipated and I responded happily with an address.[2] I told about the origins of our method and its early use with university students in Brazil; I described the way it was employed at Arizona State, the kind of results it gave us, and what our students thought about it. I suggested that the teacher of the future would no longer be a classroom entertainer, an information vendor, a critic, or debater, but would be an educational engineer—a manager of student learning.

I outlined the salient features of the system—the *unitizing* of course content; *self-pacing* of the student through the units, with *mastery* demanded at each step, but with *repeated tests* where necessary, at the hands of well-instructed and well-guided *student proctors,* without penalty in the case of failure and with maximal credit when the job was done. These elements of the system as I detailed them then are still the ones that I would stress, but we understand them better now than we did in '67.

The method is commonly known today as *PSI,* a *personalized system of instruction.* (The acronym was chosen with psychologists in mind, but *PSI* is much more frequently heard than *Psi*.) In the decade since its earliest tryout, at the University of Brasilia, its acceptance has been greater than its founders could ever have imagined[3]—not just within psychology but in other disciplines as well, at various educational levels, and in several other countries than our own.

It is my pleasant duty here to sketch the growth of PSI within its first ten years of life. I cannot do so in the detail it deserves or with justice to everyone involved. The literature on PSI is mounting daily, too rapidly for me to read or to assess, and many interesting things are taking place that may never be reported. I must deal with general impressions and in broad assertions. I will document my statements now and then, and I will try to avoid distortion of the facts, but I cannot cover everything that is known about the system or enumerate its many modifications. For the interested reader there are two good reviews of PSI research (Kulik, et al., 1974; Robin, 1974), a very good "appraisal" (Ryan, 1974), two excellent state-of-the-system papers (Cook, 1974; Ruskin, 1974), a collection of "germinal papers" (Sherman, 1974), and a handbook (Keller & Sherman, 1974) that will provide an in-depth picture of the movement (if it be that) up to the present time.

First Applications of PSI. As a method of teaching university students, PSI was first employed in a laboratory course on the analysis of behavior at the University of Brasilia in the fall of 1964. Advance descriptions of this course were written in 1963 (Keller, 1966) and 1964 (Keller, Bori, and Azzi, 1964), but the best account is the recent one by Bori (1974). A full report of the Brasilia course was never published, probably because of a brief University shutdown in 1965 which brought the young department to its end.

Two sections of a course on the analysis of behavior were taught by PSI in the spring of 1965 at Arizona State University. The results obtained in one of these became the subject matter of my talk to members of Division 2 in 1967. This report was later published under the title, "Good-bye, Teacher . . ." (Keller, 1968) and has often been cited as the recipe for PSI. The second section of the course was taught by J. G. Sherman, the other American founder of the system, with the help of a graduate teaching assistant.[4]

It required perhaps three weeks of using the method for us to realize that PSI was a good idea and would probably catch on. We had felt that it would work, long before it ever had a tryout, and we were certain that the Brasilia course must be succeeding, in spite of a chronic lack of information from that quarter. But now we had some different data—data that we hadn't seen before and which we didn't fully understand, but which was most convincing. We had only to walk into our classrooms (where students could be seen *at work*), to talk with student proctors or the graduate assistant, or to read the answers written by our pupils on their unit tests, in order to know that something educationally good was taking place. We did not feel the need for group comparisons of subject-matter mastery or the expression of approval on student questionnaires, though both were soon supplied.

Somewhat to our surprise, the acceptance or adoption of our plan by other teachers did not automatically occur. In our own Department, for example, only one professor (J. L. Michael) tried it out. A mathematics teacher came and looked, but decided that it meant a lot of work. Our Chairman and our Dean were both supportive, as was the President of the University. He arranged for us to tell about our work before a Faculty Assembly and provided a discussant from the School of Education. But our audience response was negative, to put it mildly, and we retired in some confusion to the friendlier atmosphere of students and proctors.

Word About PSI Gets Around. Gradually, through individual contacts, through papers read at meetings,[5] and through the printed word, the news began to spread and the system came to be tried out by other teachers of psychology at other institutions.[6] The results of these attempts were sufficiently rewarding to encourage its continued use by most of these hardy pioneers, often with published reports of their success. This led in turn to further tryouts, and the cycle would sometimes be repeated. From this time on, adoption of the system went ahead at growing speed and in various directions.

Among the psychologists who played a part in this extension, certain names stand out. One of these is Charles B. Ferster, whose counsel and example were important to the founding of PSI (see Keller, 1974). Ferster used a comparable procedure as early as 1967, in teaching behavior theory to graduate students at the University of Maryland. In 1968, this procedure was refined for use with undergraduates at Georgetown University and was reported as an integral part of an influential textbook on the principles of behavior (Ferster & Perrott, 1968). The method is today considered (correctly, I believe) to be a defensible form of personalized instruction. Jeffrey R. Corey and James S. McMichael (Corey & McMichael, 1974; McMichael & Corey, 1969) not only used the system in their courses, but also published a PSI companion to a well-known introductory text (Kendler, 1974), made comparisons of PSI with their prior teaching method, and generally furthered the acceptance of the system. David Born was the first to provide a teacher's and a proctor's manual for would-be users of the system. With collaborators at the University of Utah, he has made a number of investigations of PSI vis-a-vis conventional teaching (Born & Herbert, 1971; Born, et al., 1972). J. L. Michael, since his early work at Arizona State, has done much to advertise the system through lectures, consultations, and symposium participation. In his analyses of instructional techniques, Michael doesn't limit himself to PSI, but his treatment of the system has brought it to the attention of many teachers in the United States and elsewhere.

Donald Witters, Howard Gallup, and John Hess also played a part in this extension. Witters and one of his colleagues (George Kent) made evaluations of the plan, not only in psychology but in several other disciplines, at Bridgewater College (Va.), in one of the earliest studies to be funded by a governmental agency (Witters & Kent, 1970). Gallup and Hess were among the first to point up the sociological and administrative problems that may confront a teacher when he tries to fit the plan within the standard academic framework (Gallup, 1974; Hess, 1974). Hess has also been instrumental in keeping psychologists informed of what is going on with respect to PSI. He was the first to establish a clearing house for PSI materials and, with J. G. Sherman, has reported on more than 250 courses, from eleven different areas of our science (Hess & Sherman, 1972).

Other Disciplines Adopt PSI. A second line of development was the adoption of PSI in other than psychology courses, especially in physical science, engineering, and mathematics. The earliest courses were, perhaps, in electrical engineering (Pennington, 1969), introductory physics (Green, 1971), and nuclear engineering (Koen, 1970), but I am sure that there were others. A sampling of courses using PSI has twice been taken by the PSI *Newsletter,*[7] with results as shown in Table 1.

Table 1. Survey of Number of PSI Courses Offered

Subject Matter	Number of Courses	
	1972	*1974*
Psychology	73	157
Physics	38	53
Engineering	21	49
Mathematics-Statistics	20	49
Chemistry	15	31
Biology	6	21
Sociology	3	16
English	4	11
Other	10	23
Total	190	410

This listing suggests the early appeal of PSI for those whose teaching goals are well defined in terms of the knowledge or the skills to be imparted. They also show an interesting rank-order relationship on the two occasions. They do not reflect, however, either the number or the variety of courses taught today by PSI. For example, there are reported adoptions of the system in the fields of anthropology, anatomy, astronomy, accounting, art, and architecture; in biology, biochemistry, and business administration; in computer science, control systems, and conditioning; in drafting and in design; in embryology, ecology, electricity, evolution, and economics—and I am only up to F! There is hardly a field of study that can be mentioned in which someone does not use the system at one or another level of instruction. The question of keeping track of this development in any detail becomes less realistic with each day.

Broadening PSI Applications. The system is no longer limited in its application to *undergraduate* teaching. Graduate courses are becoming common, with or without the use of student proctors. (Proctor usage is not restricted to lower-level courses or courses with large enrollment; the determining factor should be the intellectual distance between the student and his teacher.) Also, the plan is found increasingly at the level of the secondary school, especially in science courses, and even further down the scale. I know of a course in Corpus Christi, Texas, wherein third-graders study arithmetic via PSI, complete with student proctors (wearing conspicuous and status-giving badges).

Within a single institution, the use of PSI may be limited to a course or two or it may extend to many. The Technological Institute of Monterrey (Mexico) has more than 60 offerings a la PSI and is gradually moving its entire curriculum in this direction. The same is said to be true of the Worcester Polytechnic Institute and the University of Wisconsin at Oshkosh, but my knowledge here is second hand.[8] The virtue of wide-scale adoption within a single department or institution lies in the possibility it provides for a student to move through all or part of a curriculum as soon as he is ready and desires to do so. In this way a college degree may be obtained in much less time than four years for many students.

PSI acceptance since 1965 now reaches well beyond the borders of Brazil or the United States. Canada and Mexico have been among the largest users of the plan (the Technological Institute of Monterrey has just been mentioned), but many others have been reported. Courses are apparently being offered in Africa, Argentina, Australia, England, India, Ireland, Israel, the Netherlands, New Zealand, Portugal, Samoa, Spain, and Tasmania, but my list again is incomplete.

Within the professions (excluding in the present context that of teaching), engineering has been the principal user of our system up till now, and some of the best examples of PSI in operation may currently be found within that field. There may be several reasons for this embracement of the plan, but one of them must surely be the work of Billy V. Koen, James E. Stice, and a group of dedicated engineering teachers at the University of Texas (Austin). Koen introduced the system there, after hearing about it from a teacher of educational psychology,[9] and has since promoted it with vigor, understanding, and imagination (Koen, 1970, 1973). Stice has been the principal agent in organizing PSI events, encouraging the plan's adoption in the University and elsewhere, and directing PSI researches (Stice, 1971). There are many other able representatives of the plan in

Texas,[10] but these two men have been outstanding from the first.

The use of PSI in medicine and related fields is just beginning, but this already seems to be an area in which the plan is sure to prosper. Recent studies from the University of Texas Health Science Center at San Antonio (Weisman & Shapiro, 1973; Nishimura, et al., 1974) and from the College of Medicine at the Ohio State University (Schimpfhauser, et al., 1974) are very encouraging with respect to the teaching of biochemistry to first-year medical students. Greatly increased subject-matter mastery is demonstrated under PSI and much wider applications are suggested. It is also noted, in the Texas study, that the proctors added an important "new dimension to the course. They acted as informal advisors to the freshmen, thereby reducing anxiety during the transition to medical school."

I hear rumors from time to time of PSI extensions beyond the academic sphere, in the training of personnel in governmental agencies and business organizations, for example. This development is to be expected, if only as a consequence of university courses in relevant areas of study where PSI may be in use, but I have no solid data to report at this time.

Research on PSI. Research carried out within the realm of PSI within the past ten years has taken several forms. The first studies to appear were those comparing PSI with lecture courses in terms of student mastery of content. I made a gesture in that direction in my initial tryout of the plan, but it was weak and unenthusiastic, coming almost as an afterthought. It seemed to me that if the superiority of the system could not be seen with "the naked eye," it was hardly worth the trouble to assess it with statistics; that the command of subject matter, although central, was no more important than other aspects of the system, say the respect for scholarship that was engendered by it; and that in a system where degree of mastery is dictated by the teacher rather than the student, something would be really wrong if less were learned.

However this may be, and however difficult the task, such comparisons have been made and reported. The general result has been well summarized by Kulik and his associates (Kulik, et al., 1974): "Content learning [under PSI] . . . is adequate. In the published studies, final examination performance in [PSI] sections always equals, and usually exceeds, performance in lecture sections." Arthur Robin, in an exhaustive study of more than a hundred PSI researches through 1973, concluded that thirteen "contrast" studies out of fifteen favored PSI (Robin, 1974).

In addition to studies such as these, there are many others—too many for adequate treatment here. Progress under PSI has been related to the attitude of the student, his prior academic standing, the amount of proctoring he receives, the size of the class to which he belongs, the number of study units in the course, the type of question on unit tests or final examinations, and so on. The effect of PSI on creativity, self-actualization, the self-image, study habits, and dropout rate has been explored. And there are studies of the causes and the treatment of *procrastination*—a problem which arises at the interface of self- and teacher-pacing. Conferences on PSI are increasingly concerned with such researches, and pressure is already building up for an interdisciplinary journal to receive them.

Support for PSI. With the growth of PSI in practice and research has come support from various public and private sources. The National Science Foundation, the Esso Educational Foundation, the Alfred P. Sloan Foundation, and other agencies and institutions have contributed in substantial fashion to the development and dissemination of the plan. The most impressive case of this to date has been the funding of a *Center for Personalized Instruction* at Georgetown University by the Fund for the Improvement of Post-Secondary Education, with additional aid from the Carnegie Corporation of New York. This Center is dedicated solely to the spread of PSI throughout the nation, through conferences and workshops, reports of courses and researches, and the collection and distribution of other useful information.

Director of the Center is J. Gilmour Sherman, one of PSI's originators, who has devoted his time increasingly to the system since 1964. Sherman is the founder of the PSI *Newsletter* and has promoted the plan throughout the United States and in Brazil, through film and lecture presentations, publication of a book of readings (Sherman, 1974), and wide-ranging participation in other PSI affairs. Co-Director of the Center is Ben A. Green, Jr., formerly of the Education Research Center at the Massachusetts Institute of Technology. Green has been a tireless worker in the furtherance of PSI throughout this country, in Latin America, and in England—perhaps in other places. He occupies a position with respect to physical-science teaching which corresponds to that of Billy Koen in engineering. Associate Director of the Center is Robert S. Ruskin, like Sherman a member of the Georgetown Psychology Department, who has been active in conducting workshops, organizing meetings, and summarizing literature on the system.

An important means of spreading PSI within the past five years has been the workshop. Hundreds of teachers have already been trained by this device to teach successful courses with the system. The workshop is sometimes operated on behalf of specific institutions as part of a teacher-development program, but more often it is open to the public on a first-come first-served basis at a standard fee. Some of the earlier workshops were limited to lectures and discussions (a not uncommon way of teaching), involving little "work" and conveying minimal know-how to the would-be user of the plan. More recently, however, PSI has been increasingly employed in *teaching* PSI.

In the summer of 1971, the National Science Foundation sponsored a two-week workshop on the plan at M.I.T. for twenty teachers, selected from a field of several hundred, drawn mainly from the Eastern seaboard. Most of them were in the field of physics, but mathematics, chemistry, biology, and sociology were also represented. Ben Green was in charge. This workshop became the model for many others, in this country and abroad.

In 1973, UNESCO brought together 35 science teachers at the University of Brasilia, where it all began. Represented in this workshop were physics, mathematics, chemistry, psychology, biology, biochemistry, and electronics. Ben Green directed the affair, aided by J. G. Sherman and C. M. Bori. The teachers came from Argentina, Brazil, Chile, Venezuela, and seven other Latin American countries. Two of the workshop courses were at the secondary-school level, three were for third- and fourth-year university students, and six were designed for higher-level teaching. Participants were later to provide reports of their courses after some experience with them. These reports were then to be made available to the other workshop members and to persons interested in UNESCO'S program in science education.

Conferences on PSI have been taking place for some time now. The first of these to deal exclusively with the system and on a national scale was organized by Green and held at M.I.T. in the autumn of 1971, under the auspices of the Education Research Center. More than 300 teachers were in attendance, from various parts of the United States and several foreign countries. The principal speakers at this two-day meeting included an astronomer (A. J. Dessler), an engineer (Billy Koen), a physicist (Edwin F. Taylor), and four psychologists (David Born, Joel Greenspoon, J. G. Sherman, and Donald Tosti). For me, the striking aspect of this conference was the display of shared experience, common purpose, and good will among men and women of widely differing backgrounds and long histories of academic insulation from one another. I decided then that PSI was not just a method of instruction or an educational movement, but a means of promoting interdisciplinary appreciation!

The most recent conference I have attended was in Washington, D. C., in April of this year. The situation there was much the same as at the one in Cambridge, but the number of those attending and the variety of interests represented were much greater. Although psychology, mathematics, chemistry, engineering, and physics dominated the program sessions, many other disciplines were included. Courses in logic, French, history, English composition, and the philosophy of education were reported, as were courses in marketing, nutrition, and business administration. Again, concern with teaching method seemed to erase the boundary lines between the different fields of study represented at this meeting.

Variations on the Theme. In the period of its existence, the identity of PSI has been maintained with some success by many teachers, occasionally in the face of serious opposition. Self-pacing, by small steps, has been possible within limits; the mastery requirement has been kept; the use of proctors has been consistently the practice, except in those high-level courses wherein a one-to-one relation of teacher to pupil could benefit both parties; and the main alternative to the grade of *A* has been the *Incomplete.* All this has been accomplished within the walls of traditional education.

However, there are countless courses in which great liberties are taken with the format. The size of the unit may be very large, the number of units very small; the limits on self-pacing may be severe, with penalties for laggards or special treats for those who keep up a certain speed; the teacher, or even a computer, may do the grading; and the final *A* may be based on factors additional to a satisfied requirement. These are just a few of the variations used, sometimes with better results than those obtained with traditional procedures, but often with unhappy outcome.

How one feels about such alterations of the system will depend upon his frame of reference. If his interest lies in educational technology and research *per se,* he will view these changes with aplomb, even as a source of new ideas. If he is administratively oriented, he may see them as desirable or essential in order to fit the new departure within the larger, well-established whole with the least amount of friction. But if he looks beyond technology and the administrative *status quo,* if he thinks of PSI as a basic paradigm of good education everywhere, he will be alarmed. He will see them (rightly, I believe) as concessions to an outmoded system and as the beginning of the end for PSI.

Future of PSI. The fate of PSI in years to come will not depend on the extermination of either of these points of view; we need technology and we need reform, and there is no good reason why they cannot work together. Nor will the future of the plan depend upon the eloquence of its supporters, the dicta of the experts, or aid from the Office of Education. It *will* depend upon the judgment of the working teacher—the one for whom the system was intended.

Such evidence as we have today makes me believe that personalized instruction is going to survive—that the teacher's verdict will be for it, and that the days of traditional group education may be numbered. I foresee some major attacks upon the plan when its impact is more widely felt and its implications are better understood, but I have no doubt about the outcome. PSI, or something very much like it, is here to stay.

Notes

1. This address, which has since been widely circulated by Individual Learning Systems of San Rafael, California, was given at the 23rd annual meeting of the American Conference of Academic Deans, on January 16, 1967.

2. The address to Division 2 was later published in the Journal of Applied Behavior Analysis (see Keller, 1968).

3. Two Brazilians (Rodolpho Azzi & Carolina Martuscelli Bori) and two Americans (J. Gilmour Sherman & myself) participated in the venture which led to PSI (see Keller, 1974).

4. A last-minute collapse of Dr. Sherman's plans to teach a special course by the PSI procedure led to a brief delay in starting this section of the introductory course, with insufficient time for recruiting proctors.

5. In addition to informal presentations at the University of Arizona and the University of Texas (Austin), papers were read by Azzi and by Keller at the Chicago meetings of the A.P.A. in 1965, by Keller at the Albuquerque meetings of the R.M.P.A. in 1966, and by Sherman at the New York meetings of the Education Research Association in 1967.

6. Among these adventurous spirits, the following names stand out: David G. Born (University of Utah), Edward S. Cobb (Barnard College), Donald A. Cook (Hunter College), Jeffrey R. Corey and James S. McMichael (C. W. Post College), Charles B. Ferster (Georgetown University), John Farmer and associates (Queens College), Howard F. Gallup (Lafayette College), John H. Hess, Jr. (Eastern Mennonite College), K. E. Lloyd and N. J. Knutzen (Washington State University), William A. Myers (University of Wisconsin), J. Russell Nazzaro (Mary Washington College), Frederick L. Newman (University of Miami), William C. Sheppard and H. G. MacDermot (University of Oregon), Gary A. Tollman (Morehouse College), and Donald R. Witters and George W. Kent (Bridgewater College). In brief, my son-in-law, six former pupils, and some friends (or friends of friends), plus two or three strangers whose work I heard of later. New teaching methods are examined on a purely rational, strictly impersonal basis!

7. The *Personalized System of Instruction Newsletter,* founded in June of 1971 by Sherman, at Georgetown University, and since then issued quarterly, provides an excellent picture, in its contents and its subscription list, of the PSI development within the past four years.

8. EPIE Report No. 61, volume 7, April 1974 (Educational Products Information Exchange, 463 West St., New York, N. Y. 10014) contains an informative and insightful account of PSI by one of its early users, Donald A. Cook, now of the Psychology Department of Queens College (CUNY).

9. Luiz F. S. Natalicio, now of the School of Education, McMurry College, Texas. Dr. Natalicio became acquainted with PSI when he was engaged in Peace Corps training at Arizona State University in 1966.

10. Important members of the original group at the University of Texas (Austin) were L. L. Hoberock (mechanical engineering), C. H. Roth, Jr. (electrical engineering), and G. R. Wagner (operations research), but they were quickly joined by others—e.g., W. T. Fowler & P. E. Nacozy (engineering statics), and B. G. Herring (library science). In psychology and education, Carl F. and Susan McF. Hereford have been especially helpful in promotion and in research on PSI evaluation. Outside of Austin, A. J. Dessler (space science, Rice University), G. F. Paskusz (Associate Dean, Cullen School of Engineering, University of Houston), and R. A. Weisman (biochemistry, Health Science Center, University of Texas, San Antonio) have been especially influential in furthering PSI.

References

Bori, C. M. Developments in Brazil. In: F. S. Keller & J. G. Sherman, *The Keller Plan handbook: Essays on a personalized system of instruction.* Menlo Park, CA: W. A. Benjamin, Inc., 1974.

Born, D. G., & Herbert, E. A further study of personalized instruction in large university classes. *Journal of Experimental Education,* 1971, *40,* 6-11.

Born, D. G., Gledhill, S. M., & Davis, M. L. Examination performance in lecture-discussion and personalized instruction courses. *Journal of Applied Behavior Analysis,* 1972, 5, 3-43.

Cook, D. A. Personalized system of instruction: Potential and problems. EPIE Report No. 61, vol. 7, 1974. Educational Products Information Exchange, 2-13.

Corey, J. R., & McMichael, J. S. Retention in a PSI introductory psychology course. In J. G. Sherman (Ed.), *Personalized system of instruction: 41 germinal papers.* Menlo Park, CA: W. A. Benjamin, Inc., 1974, 17-19.

Ferster, C. B. Individualized instruction in a large introductory psychology course. *Psychological Record,* 1968, *18,* 521-532.

Ferster, C. B., & Perrott, M. C. *Behavior principles.* New York: Appleton-Century-Crofts, 1968.

Gallup, H. F. Problems in the implementation of a course in personalized instruction. In J. G. Sherman (Ed.), *Personalized system of instruction: 41 germinal papers.* Menlo Park, CA: W. A. Benjamin, Inc., 1974.

Green, B. A., Jr. Physics teaching by the Keller Plan at M.I.T. *American Journal of Physics.* 1971, *39,* 764-775.

Hess, J. H., Jr. Keller Plan instruction: Implementation problems. In J. G. Sherman (Ed.), *Personalized system of instruction: 41 germinal papers.* Menlo Park, CA: W. A. Benjamin, Inc., 1974, 137-147.

Hess, J. H., Jr., & Sherman, J. G. *PSI psychology course catalog.* Harrisonburg, Va.: PSI Clearing House, Eastern Mennonite College, 1972.

Keller, F. S. A personal course in psychology. In R. Ulrich, T. Stachnik, & J. Mabry (Eds.), *Control of Human Behavior.* Glenview, IL: Scott Foresman, 1966, 91-93.

Keller, F. S. "Good-bye, Teacher . . ." *Journal of Applied Behavior Analysis,* 1968, *1,* 79-89.

Keller, F. S. An international venture in behavior modification. In F. S. Keller & E. Ribes-Inesta (Eds.), *Behavior modification: Applications to education.* New York: Academic Press, 1974.

Keller, F. S., Bori, C. M., & Azzi, R. Um curso moderno de psicologia. *Ciencia e cultura,* 1964, *16,* 397-399.

Keller, F. S., & Sherman, J. G. *The Keller Plan handbook: Essays on a personalized system of instruction.* Menlo Park, CA: W. A. Benjamin, Inc., 1974.

Kendler, H. H. *Basic psychology* (3rd ed.). Menlo Park, CA: W. A. Benjamin, Inc., 1974.

Koen, B. V. Self-paced instruction for engineering students. *Engineering Education,* 1970, *60,* 735-736.

Koen, B. V. Determining the unit structure in a PSI course. *Engineering Education,* 1973, *63,* 432-434.

Kulik, J. A., Kulik, C-L, & Carmichael, K. The Keller Plan in science teaching. *Science,* 1974, *183,* 379-383.

McMichael, J. S., & Corey, J. R. Contingency management in an introductory psychology course produces better learning. *Journal of Applied Behavior Analysis,* 1969, *2,* 79-83.

Nishimura, J. S., Rees, A. W., Shapiro, D. M., & Weisman, R. A. Medical school biochemistry: what the proctors told us. Paper presented at the National Conference on Personalized Instruction in Higher Education, Washington, D. C., April 5-6, 1974.

Pennington, P. R. A teaching innovation: The "Keller Plan." Report to the Dean of Undergraduate Studies, Portland State University, Portland, OR, Aug. 4, 1969.

Robin, A. *Behavioral instruction in the classroom: A review.* Stony Brook, N.Y.: State University of New York Instructional Resources Center, Technical Publication No. C-1-74, 1974.

Ruskin, R. S. The personalized system of instruction: An educational alternative. ERIC/Higher Education Research Report No. 5, 1974.

Ryan, B. A. *Keller's personalized system of instruction: An appraisal.* Washington, D.C.: American Psychological Association, 1974.

Schimpfhauser, F., Horrocks, L., Richardson, K., Alben, J., Schumm, D., & Sprecher, H. The personalized program of instruction as an adaptable alternative within the traditional structure of medical basic sciences. Paper presented at the National Conference on Personalized Instruction in Higher Education, Washington, D.C., April 5-6, 1974.

Sherman, J. G. (Ed.). *Personalized system of instruction: 41 germinal papers.* Menlo Park, CA: W. A. Benjamin, Inc., 1974.

Stice, J. E. (Ed.). *The personalized system of instruction: The Keller plan applied in engineering education.* Bulletin No. 4, December 1971, Bureau of Engineering Teaching, College of Engineering, University of Texas at Austin.

Weisman, R. A., & Shapiro, D. M. Personalized system of instruction (Keller Method) for medical school biochemistry. *Journal of Medical Education,* 1973, *48,* 934-938.

Witters, D. R., & Kent, G. W. An experimental evaluation of programming student study behavior in undergraduate courses. Research project under Health, Education, and Welfare grant 9-C-040, 1970, Bridgewater College, Bridgewater, VA.

13

Psychologists and Educators

In the preface to this book, I listed some discoveries I had made while examining my published papers and my speeches. Two more findings may be noted here, neither of which should be surprising to the reader. I found that I was not a laboratory man—not the sort of experimental scientist I had idealized and sometimes thought myself to be. I was, instead, a species of behavioral engineer—an applied behavior analyst, if you will, or a "behavior modifier" (I never really liked the term).

Also, I became an *educator*! With the spread of personalized instruction to other disciplines than my own, to other universities, and into other lands, I became expansive. I began to think about the plight of teaching everywhere, not just in my own classes; I began to make pronouncements that went far beyond my data; and, lacking any checkrein, I made some bold assertions.

Instances of the latter can be found in this final paper. It was delivered as an opening address to The International Conference on New Methods in University Education, held in Xalapa, Mexico, at the University of Vera Cruz, on November 3-7, 1975.

In the autumn of 1936, I attended the 44th Annual Meeting of the American Psychological Association. The meeting was held at Dartmouth College, in Hanover, New Hampshire. Clark Hull, one of America's best-known behaviorists of that time, was President of the Association. All young rebels against the mentalism of our day felt obligated to attend.

While I was at this meeting a friend of mine suggested that we visit the Baker Memorial Library on the campus to see the famous murals that had been completed there just two years before. The name of the painter who had done the work was Jose Clemente Orozco.

One fresco in particular attracted my attention when we got there, and I examined it for some time, trying to get its message. It pictured a delivery room, in which a child was being born, but it was a very unusual childbirth scene. Everyone attending was dressed in cap and gown, such as professors sometimes wear, and each was a skeleton or, perhaps, a mummy. The mother was a skeleton, and so was the child, who wore an academic cap. The panel was entitled *Alma Mater.*

After the meetings had ended, my friend went back to his laboratory and I went back to my classroom. It took me thirty years to understand that his laboratory and my classroom were intimately related, and that both of us were far behind Orozco in our recognition of the most important problem of our time.

I refer to the problem of effective education, with which this Conference is concerned. It seems to me now that most of the evils of our society are related to its absence, and that some of our greatest goods depend upon its presence.

I have no right to speak for Mexico in this connection, but I can tell you with considerable assurance that formal education in my country is in serious trouble. This is true at every level, from the grade school to the graduate school, and for every branch of learning.

Some of our educational institutions have already had to close their doors; others are soon expected to do the same, especially at the private college level. Some of these are merging within consortiums, for economic reasons. All of them, without exception, are trying to reduce their costs of operation. The public appeal and public support of higher education has diminished. Once-powerful administrators have lost a great deal of their status, as well as their source of income. Teachers are finding themselves with an uncertain academic future. Some of them have already had to take a salary reduction, and others are without employment. Everyone has been affected in one way or another.

In April of this year, I attended a conference of university trustees, at which many colleges and universities were represented from all over the United States. The principal speaker at this meeting was Dr. Clark Kerr, formerly President of the University of California (discharged by Governor Reagan in 1967, and made President Emeritus in 1974). Dr. Kerr is said to be our most influential figure in higher education.

Student enrollment was the principal concern of Dr. Kerr in his address, and he took what he called an "optimistic point of view." He predicted a "steady state" in university admissions for the next three decades, with an average growth rate of *one percent per year* in student population. This "optimistic" viewpoint was supported by a large amount of data, collected by the Carnegie Council on Policy Studies in Higher Education, by the U. S. Office of Education, and other prestigious organizations. Most of the projections examined by Dr. Kerr were less optimistic than his.

Dr. Kerr had some suggestions with respect to what we ought to do in order to survive. He said we should reconsider our goals, and put more emphasis on practical matters in our teaching. He told us to pay more attention to the rules of collective bargaining and the granting of faculty tenure. He urged us to look for students in unusual places—among the high-school drop-outs and those who never attended high school; among gifted high-school juniors, who often waste their senior year; and from the adult population, where an interest in more education is commonly reported. He said we ought to seek new leaders—presidents, for example, who would act like merchants, looking for new customers, advertising their products, and the like. His final bit of counsel was to keep our eyes upon the future, on the year 2000, when the buildings we constructed in the sixties would be paid for, when the teachers whom we hired at that time would be gone, and when the birthrate might have settled down. Dr. Kerr did not suggest, nor did any other speaker whom I heard, that we improve our methods of teaching. He did not say that a satisfied customer is the best advertisement for a business, or that inferior products are often signs of future failure.

Various explanations have been offered, by Dr. Kerr and others, of the unhappy state of our colleges and universities today. Among those commonly mentioned are the war in Vietnam, the inflation of our money, the recognition of minority groups in our society, the increased use of drugs among our youth, and changes in our sexual morality. These explanations, taken singly or together, do not entirely satisfy. They may have been important in precipitating matters—in triggering a reaction—but the basic reason lies much deeper.

If we accept the proposition that the purpose of higher education is to transmit the essence of our culture—our accumulated knowledge and our skills—from one generation to the next, I think it must be said that we have failed. With a small percentage of our students, we may claim to be successful; they are the source of our supply of scientists, technologists, and scholars. *Many* of those whom we profess to teach, however, are in a worse condition, morally and mentally, when they leave our institutions than they were at the time they entered. They have little competence, self-reliance, or respect for learning; they are often aimless and confused, cynical and disillusioned; they are vulnerable to quacks and demagogues, to superstition and bizarre religions. They have survived within the system for reasons unrelated to scholarly achievement or well-mastered skills.

I hope it is understood that I am talking about conditions in the United States, as I perceive them. I cannot speak for those in Mexico or elsewhere with the same assurance. It is my distinct impression that the situation in this country is not as bad as in my own, and that your future is somewhat brighter than is ours, possibly because you haven't yet managed to make so many blunders; but I would rather not be quoted at this time as having said that the educational system here could not be better.

Our North American colleges and universities have failed through their neglect of the very problem with which this conference is concerned. For many years they have occupied themselves with questions of *whom* we ought to teach, *what* we ought to teach, *when, where,* and even *why* we ought to teach, but almost never with the question *how.* Yet this is a central question the answer to which may also affect our answers to the others; and it is the only question of the list which deals with the behavior of the student, the one we all pretend to serve.

Group instruction by the lecture method has been our anwer to the *how* of education since 1638, when Comenius published his *Great Didactic.* The method was bad at that time, but it is worse today, because it is more widely used. Increasingly it has led our university students to lie, to steal, to cheat, to bribe, to plagiarize, and to behave in other immoral ways. It has led our teachers to engage in showmanship, in tyranny, or in courting the favor of their pupils. It has encouraged self-deception, compromise of principle, and dishonesty. It is responsible for most of the low esteem in which the teaching craft is regarded by the public.

The system has endured, perhaps, because we had a lot of money and natural resources; we could afford to waste our talent. Or perhaps because the teachers made other contributions to society that were more important than their teaching. Or perhaps it was because we thought that nothing could be done to improve the situation. But now the system is in trouble. The need for change becomes more pressing every day. It is time to reexamine, in the light of modern science, the teaching methods we employ.

In 1936, when my friend and I went to see Orozco's paintings, there was no understanding of human conduct as we know of it today. Any educator at that time who went to a psychologist to improve his teaching would be only wasting time. He might hear about a few experiments on forgetting, on movements of the eyes while reading, on transfer of training, or on some other matters of interest to researchers of that period. But the practical usefulness of anything he heard would have been extremely small.

Since those days, however, a science of behavior has emerged, with technologies based upon it. Laws of learning are now well known and may be put to work in many places, including those of education. It pleases me to note at this time that the man who shaped this science, who guided its development through its early stages, and who applied its laws to several spheres of thought and action, was the friend whom I have mentioned—B. F. Skinner. Without his genius, and his efforts in behalf of education, many of us would not be at this meeting.

The area of basic science that we owe to Skinner is generally referred to as the *experimental analysis of behavior*. It is a derivative of Skinner's system of 1938—*reinforcement theory*. The technology that Skinner introduced is commonly called *behavior modification* or, less frequently, *applied behavior anlaysis*.

Behavior modification has its roots in reinforcement theory and experimental science, but its goals are practical and humanistic, requiring a special attitude and special skills. It has its textbooks and its journals and its professional meetings. Several universities already give advanced degrees within this rapidly expanding field, and centers have been founded for both research and practice. Institutes and schools of behavior modification are probably just around the corner. Several well-known leaders in this movement, from both sides of the border, are with us here today.

When I was told about the purpose of this conference, I asked myself a simple question: What can the educator learn from the psychologist at such a meeting? More specifically, what can a reinforcement theorist or a behavior modifier say that would be useful to anyone involved in planning or directing university education? The answer that I arrived at had three parts.

First of all, he can supply a behavioral analysis of the teaching process. He is able to relate what takes place in any classroom to the principles of learning that derive from laboratory science. This could be his most important function, since a rationale is thus provided for the acceptance or rejection of any teaching practice or proposal. The work of J. L. Michael in this field has been outstanding, and I look ahead with interest to his contribution to this program.

Secondly, the behavior modifier can suggest a variety of procedures that may be useful in research or as practical devices for dealing with classroom and related problems. The *Journal of Applied Behavior Analysis* is a well-known source of such techniques. I expect to find a number of examples

166

among the studies to be reported here within the next four days.

Thirdly, there are comprehensive teaching systems which have their roots in reinforcement theory and provide a radical departure from traditional education. One of these, the *personalized system of instruction,* or *PSI,* is a plan that I have tried to further since its earliest days. Unlike the special devices of my second category, this way of teaching doesn't easily fit within the traditional format. It does, however, eliminate many of the evils of the classical system and is in excellent accord with a democratic approach to higher education. It lets the student move through any course of study individually and privately, at his own rate, but with accountability at every step; it provides for guidance and encouragement from a well-instructed peer; it relies upon the printed or the written, rather than the spoken, word; it employs the lecture only as a source of inspiration; and it gives to every student equal credit when the work has been completed.

From what I have said thus far it should be clear that I believe our present system of higher education fails to meet the needs of modern life, and that it really does more harm than good. It should also be apparent that, in my opinion, the behavior modifier, the applied behavior analyst, the educational psychologist, or whatever you may call him, is able to improve this situation. An analysis of teaching method has been made; a technology for dealing with special teaching problems now exists; and at least one alternative to group instruction has been formulated and applied with some success. All this is true, I think, but it is not enough.

The missing element in the picture is the *delivery system.* The most acute analysis, the most refined procedures of research or practice, the best alternative to the traditional system—these have very little value unless they are accessible to those who need them. The surest remedy for a disease can do no good unless it reaches the patient.

Behavior modifiers have no power (indeed, they have no right) to impose their will upon the educational organization. Their activities are determined, or restricted, by the institutions that they serve, whether it be the prison, the mental hospital, the school, or any other. Their goals may be humanistic, but they work for pay; they are essentially employees and they cannot dictate—they cannot "call the shots." They cannot say what shall, or shall not, be adopted by these institutions.

Heads of colleges and universities also have less power to produce a change than is commonly supposed. Their faculties may be reluctant to accept the new departure; their governing boards—their trustees, their regents, their directors—may place limits on their freedom; and even students have been known to resent administrative *fiat.*

I do not know the best solution to this problem. Currently we attack on many fronts. With money from government agencies or private foundations, we set up conferences like this one to let influential educators know about our work. We give workshops for instruction in the new technique or system; we write articles for journals, both technical and popular, to help in spreading the word throughout the land; and, especially, we give speeches everywhere we can. But we have no focal point of contact, no single interface, with the educational establishment, whereby our technology can be assessed and brought to bear directly on the education of our youth.

For awhile I thought that the departments and the schools of education would be the answer to this problem. In the early days of PSI, I thought we would arouse much interest there, and I even worried about encroachment on their province. I quickly learned, however, that (with rare exceptions) they too were more concerned with other matters than the techniques of instruction at the university level.

Sometimes I get discouraged. The need for better teaching is so urgent and our progress seems to be so slow. Education is so basic to the survival of mankind, and our time is running out. Anarchy and chaos are standing at the schoolhouse door, with no one there to bar the way.

Then I think about our progress since 1936, in behavior science and its applications, and some of my hope returns. In the past ten years alone, we have learned more about the *how* of education than in the previous three hundred. If Jose Clemente Orozco were alive today and given the commission to paint another *Alma Mater,* at least the newborn baby might be given flesh and blood—might have some living tissue on those little bones.

There was another question that I asked myself when I heard about this meeting. What will be the educator's contribution? Or, to say this in another way, what can the psychologist learn from the administrator or the teacher here—the ones whom he desires to serve?

In answering this, I tried to find some simple parallels to the relationship that might exist. I thought of the behavior modifier as a burglar, preparing to rob a home by studying in advance the structure of the house and the routine movements of its occupant, the educator. Then I fancied the behavior modifier as a fireman, called to help the educator put out the schoolhouse fire. I also imagined him as a salesman, knocking at the door and trying to sell his wares to the lady of the house—the educator.

But there was something wrong with all of these comparisons, as well as others that I thought of. A burglar has minimal interest in the welfare of those within the house he plans to rob, and the owner of the house is unlikely to cooperate in the crime; the fireman sometimes does a lot of damage while putting out the fire; and the salesman often tries to sell the housewife things she doesn't really need, or cannot afford. And so on.

So I gave up similes in favor of the following suggestion. Before the

168

applied behavior analyst can be effective in serving the needs of the educational institution, he ought to understand in detail its current mode of operation. He ought to know what changes in the system may recently have been made, or are in progress; he should know what obstacles he may encounter and what restrictions may be placed upon his function, if he attempts to make a major or a minor innovation. Some of this knowledge can be assumed because he, himself, is a teacher, or has been one, but not all. There are many relevant matters of which he is probably unaware, but matters concerning which the educator has detailed information. The practical educator can tell the practical psychologist a lot of things he ought to know.

The psychologist and the educator have a common goal: the improvement of education in our time. Each one wants to be effective and respected for his efforts, but not at the other's expense. Without the aid of the educator (the administrator or the working teacher), the psychologist (the applied behavior analyst or the behavior modifier) works within a vacuum; without the aid of the psychologist, the educator cannot realize his full potential.

The educator who attends this conference simply to meet with other educators or to strengthen his defenses against those who may want to change his way of life sometime in the future, is missing an important opportunity; and the behavior analyst who comes here to listen to other behavior analysts, under very pleasant circumstances, and sees the educator as the enemy of progress, is missing even more. This conference should provide an excellent point of contact, a golden opportunity for communication between representatives of the new technology and the establishment it pretends to serve.